Tales from the We

Alan Thomas

To my uncle Islwyn and former neighbours and friends Glyndwr and David who were sadly taken before their time.

CONTENTS

PHOTOGRAPHS AND MAPS

Introduction

I have thought of writing a book for some time especially after regaling my grand children with stories from my childhood. Following suggestions from my son in law George that I should, the corona virus pandemic, which hit the country in the spring of 2020, gave me the time and opportunity to do so. Lockdown started in March 2020 and was considerably eased during the summer months, but as the book comes to its conclusion in September, restrictions are being re-imposed and I suspect that we are heading for another lockdown.

This book, I hope, describes what it was like growing up in the countryside in West Wales in the 1950s and 1960s although in places it does stray into later years. It is centred on our family when we lived in Brynislwyn, about four miles south of the old market town of Cardigan or Aberteifi in Welsh. However it also features heavily three other families, our immediate neighbours the Richards family of Wenvoe Farm and westwards slightly further away the Allisons of Sychpant Farm and the Edwards family of Rhiwgoi, a small cottage a few hundred yards away in the other direction. Each family had children who were our close friends and thus we spent a lot of time together. The book would have been much diminished without significant contributions from Mary Slade (formerly Richards of Wenvoe), Tony Edwards of Rhiwgoi and especially Jean Jones, the eldest of the Allison children of Sychpant. There were also contributions from my brother, Lyndon and sister Brenda, and Jean's siblings Cathy and John. I am also grateful to dad's cousin's daughter Wendy Lewis for information which helped make the chapter on Blaenffos Church more complete. My wife Joanne's map making and IT skills were invaluable. I am also lucky that my parents, Idris ninety-seven and Morfydd ninety-six at the time of writing, are still going strong and were able to provide a great deal of valuable information. Finally thanks go to my daughter Rachel who checked over everything before it went for publication. I am very grateful to all the contributors. I should stress again that the book is largely based on the recollections of mostly myself, but also of the contributors mentioned and we all know that the mind can behave strangely and mysteriously so I apologise in advance for any errors it may contain.

In West Wales, where the phrase 'you're not from around here are you' is common, it's quite usual to refer to people by their first name and occupation or place of residence; hence you will come across names like Brynley Wenvoe, Jack Wenvoe, John Sychpant, Jimmy Rhiwgoi, Evan Gof, Jim Rhyd, Wyn Penlanbrydell, John Cwmbettws, Dan Trip, Norman and Sally Foundry, John Car Parts and Cilgerran based pet food supplier Dave Dog Food who, according to my father, has the biggest nuts in the area.

The map on the next page shows the location of towns, villages and beaches which are featured in the book. It shows the Pembrokeshire and Cardigan Bay coast between Fishguard and Llangrannog as well as the route of the Cardi Bach, the section of the Carmarthen to Cardigan railway line which ran from Whitland to Cardigan.

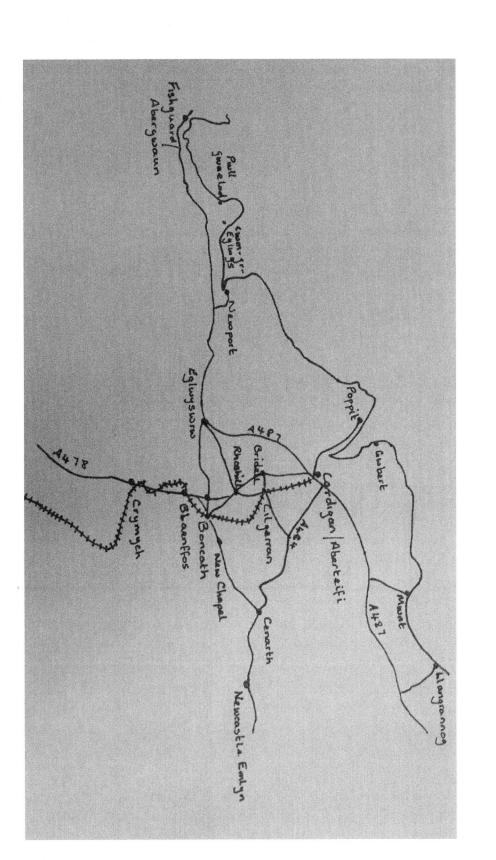

Cardigan/Aberteifi

I was born in 1950 at the hospital in Cardigan, a small market town on the coast in West Wales. In Elizabethan times it was one of the most important ports in Wales and in the 1800s it became one of the major ports in the United Kingdom. Hundreds of ships were built on the Teifi and they carried a range of goods all over the world. At one time it was a major departure point for emigration to the USA and Canada but by the start of the twentieth century it had declined significantly. Today it is regarded by the Times as one of the best places to live in Wales, however it was a little different in the 1950s, but still a great place to live. It had a railway station (this was before the Beaching cuts), a thriving livestock market, a cinema, a castle and some lovely river fronts. On the south side of the town there was a narrow bridge, on which two cars could just about pass, which linked the two sides of the River Teifi. It carried the A487, the road which ran from Fishguard to the west, to Cardigan and along the Cardigan Bay coast to Aberystwyth and onto Caernarfon and the Menai Bridge, in North Wales, which links the mainland to Anglesey. Today this old bridge is still busy but there is an alternative crossing over another bridge to the east which carries the Cardigan by-pass over the river.

The streets and buildings have changed very little. As with any town there has been a turnover of shops and other premises. There are now more coffee shops, cafes and other businesses that are geared towards tourism. There are quaint alleyways which reveal a variety of small specialist traders. There's still a shop selling carpets and furniture but department stores like Bon Marche have closed and Woolworths has gone, however the building is now occupied by a branch of The Original Factory Shop. The cinema has gone but there is now a relatively new and thriving centre called Theatre Mwldan which puts on a range of entertainment including films, plays, concerts and even ballet, plus musical and comedy acts. There is also a swimming pool and a leisure centre.

There is a well preserved guildhall and a market hall which were built in the 1850s out of slate from the nearby Cilgerran quarries. Outside this building there was and still is a cannon given to the town in 1857 in memory of soldiers from the area that were killed in the Crimean War. Apparently it was used during the famous charge of the light brigade. Many of the pubs are still in existence. The Black Lion is still doing good trade but gone is the Saturday night dance which was held upstairs and could usually guarantee a punch up before the night was out. There are also many out of town stores now, along the bypass, like Tesco, B & M Bargains and Aldi as well as a couple of small industrial estates with retail and wholesale units.

The Family/Teulu

We were a family of five: mam, dad, my older brother Lyndon and younger sister Brenda. In the early years my mother's father lived with us but he died before my sister was born. I recently had a chat with my mother (born in 1923 and physically a little frail, much to her annoyance, but mentally as sharp as ever) about our time as children and she felt that they were quite strict (reasonably so) and sometimes cruel (never). I told her that I could only remember happy times. Looking back now, dad did meet out the occasional bit of physical punishment but I know that each time I deserved it as I could be a naughty little bugger. One time I was in trouble for something and I'd escaped to the top of the stairs. Dad was telling me what he was going to do to me when he got hold of me. So I said 'come up here and say that' and when he started up the stairs I ran into my bedroom and locked the door. He tells me now that he hadn't started up the stairs but merely banged his feet on the bottom step to make me think he was coming, something that many parents have done, I'm sure. I know I have and apparently my wife's mother used to bang a coat hanger on the bottom of the stairs as the children escaped. I stayed in my room for a little while in the hope that he would cool down which of course he had done straight away.

We were poor, it was just after the war, there was still food rationing but we as children weren't aware of this, there always seemed to be food on the table. We were lucky that we had grounds and that we lived in the countryside. We were able to grow a lot of our own food, we could go foraging in the countryside for fruit, we kept chickens and we could get milk from the farm next door. There was a lot of home cooking, baking, jam and chutney making and home-made wine and non alcoholic drinks all made from ingredients grown or foraged. Elderberry and elderflower wine were particular favourites.

Summer 1957, standing on the pavement in Cilgerran waiting for the carnival procession to pass by.

I was born a year after my brother and since my parents couldn't afford two cots, my bed was a drawer taken out of a large chest of drawers. For years I thought they would slide the drawer, with me in it, back into the chest overnight! As we grew up we were good friends but there was always a bit of a rivalry between us. As I was always smaller than him I would always come off worse in any physical altercation that we might have, but god help anyone else who tried to have a go at me. My sister came along six years later and, having two older brothers, ended up a real tomboy. She would have played rugby like her brothers if she was a teenager today, but she had to make do with hockey. She became a Welsh International at school girl, adult and veteran levels and now, into her sixties, she is still playing regularly. During the 1950s however I don't remember much about my sister featuring in our lives. I was nine in

1959, my brother was ten and my sister was three. I doubt that two lively robust boys would want much to do with a three year old girl.

The House and Grounds

We were extremely lucky to live in the countryside, we had free run of fields roads, woods, country tracks, we could wonder off for hours without our parents becoming concerned. We lived in a house surrounded by farmland, we had a lot of grounds which we made full use of to play in, grow crops and keep a few animals for extra income. At various times we had Corgis, Pekingese, chickens and pigs.

The house we lived in was built in 1908; it had thick solid stone walls built with stones of various size and thickness with soil rather than cement in between. The floor was made of blue flagstones laid on soil and they always seemed well worn to me after nearly fifty years of use. Each room had a small sash window, the beams were exposed, and there was no plaster board ceilings, just floor boards laid upstairs onto the beams. The roof was made out of blue Caernarvon slate. It was a good size with 4 bedrooms and a junk room (later to become my bedroom) upstairs but no indoor bathroom or toilet. Baths were taken in a tin bath in front of the kitchen fire. The outside toilet was out of the back door, up some steps and up a garden path to the top of the vegetable garden. It was a two seater, one adult and one child size cut out of a plank of wood – painted so we wouldn't get splinters. There were two large buckets and cut up newspaper hanging on a string for toilet paper. When the buckets were full it was dad's job to bury the waste in the garden, no wonder the vegetable crops were so good. Composting toilets are now considered green; so we were clearly ahead of our time! In reality, of course, we were just the same as the majority of other households. A journey to the toilet was a pretty cold and scary affair in the dark winter evenings, but once inside the zinc hut it was quite cosy.

The kitchen was the focus of the house; it had a very old cast iron fireplace, with a chain and hook to hang the kettle over the fire. We would burn wood, of which there was a plentiful supply in the garden, and coal. When the coal man came my brother and I had to stand over him and count the sacks as they emptied them in the coal shed because dad didn't trust them to leave the number ordered. The fireplace had an oven and there was a separate plank, as we used to call it, which you could place over the top of the fire like a hot plate. Saucepans could be placed on this when it got really hot and it was great for making pancakes and blackberry clamp over. This is a bit like a tart except you have a circular piece of pastry; you cover one half with blackberries and loads of sugar, fold over the other half and seal it by pressing down around the edges a la Mary Berry. The juices inevitably seeped out but eaten fresh it was gorgeous and it wasn't bad cold the next day either. Above the fireplace there was a clothes airer which was raised and lowered using a pulley system. This was well used during wet weather to dry and to air clothes; in fact it seemed to have clothes on it most of the time. There was an enamel bowl for washing up and an old ceramic Belfast sink, some cupboards, a dining table and chairs and some kind of couch covered in green vinyl which looked like a modern day chaise longue. It also had an oak Welsh settle which is a long bench with a back and arms usually with storage space under the seat which can be lifted and is designed to seat several people.

We had no fridge, no freezer and certainly no television. We did have electricity and I discovered much later that dad had fitted most of the power points and lighting which would explain all the cables running along the walls. It certainly wouldn't meet current safety regulations or even those that existed at the time I bet. Although he's now in his late nineties he still likes to fit additional plugs and lights! At the back of the house there was quite a cold room, (actually the whole house away from the kitchen was pretty cold), called the **llaethdy** (literally translated it means milk house but the nearest thing today would be the utility room/pantry) where we had what we called a safe. This was a small cupboard made by my uncle Trevor out of hardboard with a mesh door to keep the flies out in which we kept fresh food, including milk. The milk was collected every day in a jug from the farm next door and as milking was twice a day there was no problem if we ran out. The **llaethdy** also housed the washing machine, there was no spinner but a mangle sat on top of the machine which you had to wind by hand. This was basically two rollers through which you would pass the wet washing which would come out the other side as flat as a pancake and dry enough to hang on the washing line outside or on the airer in the kitchen.   I also remember sides of salted ham and bacon hanging from hooks attached to the beams.   The salt and the cold would be enough to preserve them so they would last for a few months.   This probably explains why bacon and egg was a regular meal in our house.

Of the two other rooms downstairs, one was used as an everyday sitting room when we weren't in the kitchen, and the last room was a 'best' only sitting room for important guests which was used no more than half a dozen times a year.   It had a nice three piece suite, some smart rugs and a glass display cabinet.   Around Christmas time my dad's brother and family would come over and the grownups would be in the best sitting room and the children would be in the everyday lounge, which suited us, just fine.   Both rooms had open fires, the one in the everyday living room was regularly lit and the other was occasionally lit; it certainly was at Christmas. They both faced north and had fabulous views of the countryside towards Cardigan and the coast of Cardigan Bay.   On a good day you could even see North Wales. Between these two rooms there was a corridor which led to the front door, wider than today's standard sized doors with a glass panel above on which was inscribed the name of the house, Brynislwyn, and the year it was built, 1908.

In the late 1950s there were two major changes which made a huge difference to our lives. The first was the installation of an indoor bathroom and toilet.   It was installed in the bedroom above the kitchen which meant it was nice and warm most of the time. It also had an airing cupboard, which dad built out of wood and hardboard, which contained an un-lagged hot water cylinder which also helped to keep it nice and warm.   A slight drawback was that the window had standard clear glass so you had to make sure you drew the curtain if using the toilet, not that there were often people outside in that part of the garden. Dad did much of the work himself and was helped with the plumbing by the local smithy (known as Ianto Gof) and his assistant Leslie (who was our cousin) who were also welders. One of the biggest jobs was digging a cesspit. As the location had to be close to the house (it was dug out on the bank at the pine end of the house) it wasn't accessible by machinery so had to be dug by hand and all the soil, stones and clay moved elsewhere by wheelbarrow. Fortunately there was plenty of room in the grounds to dump them. It was also fortunate that being on a bank there wasn't much water in the bottom as it was dug out. Finally a trench had to be dug around the side of the house to carry the wastepipe to the cesspit.

I have fond memories of the airing cupboard; it was always lovely and warm and was used to store our clothes and spare bedding. More than once I ended up sleeping on the bedding on the middle shelf as I couldn't sleep in the bed I shared with my brother due to his snoring. I could still hear it through the wall but it wasn't loud enough to stop me sleeping. Our bedroom was a good size and was (in estate agents speak) dual aspect with two windows. It contained just a bed and a wardrobe. The bed was quite old with a lumpy mattress on springs and it used to dip in the middle so we were forever grabbing the side of the mattress to prevent ourselves rolling into the middle and (heaven forbid) actually touch each other. Lyndon still slept in this room when he came home from university but by then there was a new bed. Being a student he used to jam his socks in the window overnight so that he could get two days use out of them. Eventually I got my own room, the small room at the back which had been used as a store room. Dad fitted a wardrobe across one end and together with a single bed that's all I needed. I think that it was probably the coldest room in the house being away from the kitchen and above the llaethdy but with plenty of bedding pulled over my head I was soon warm as toast. We didn't have any hot water bottles and my feet were always cold, so I would pull my pyjama bottoms down far enough that the bottom could be tucked under my feet to warm them up. The slight disadvantage of this was a cold bottom. I suppose I should have gone to the airing cupboard when it was very cold!

The second major change was to take out the old fireplace in the kitchen and replace it with a Rayburn stove and cooker which was fed by both logs and coal. This heated the water in the hot water cylinder and the oven and hotplate made cooking a lot easier, but there was no central heating. Not long after this it was decided to replace the blue slate stone floors with concrete and Jimmy Rhiwgoi did a lot of the work with dad's help and for the first time a damp course of thick plastic sheeting was put down under the concrete screed. The stones were about fifty years old when replaced and they had worn away to become uneven with constant use over this time. Of course today such floors would be a valuable asset in old character housing.

During the 1960s several other changes occurred, most involved more concreting. The first part to be concreted over was the entrance, drive and area around the sheds. This was a very large section and took a long time. Dad did it mostly himself but I was a very willing helper and I would often ask 'what are we doing today dad?' The concrete section in front of the shed made a perfect tennis court with a much more even bounce than the old dirt drive and with an improvised net we spent a lot of time playing tennis especially during the summer months. The next section to be done was the path up to the house and the small yard along the back of the house. As the concrete was mixed down by the shed this involved a fair amount of transporting as we did the back of the house first and then the top of the path working downwards. Fortunately, or probably unfortunately, we had an old wheelbarrow made entirely of iron (even the wheel), which was pretty heavy even when empty and was quite difficult to push despite the liberal use of oil on the iron wheel. The only way to do it was to fit a harness at the front which I fitted into and pulled while dad had the handles and pushed.

One improvement which dad resisted for a long time was loft insulation as he was convinced that it made little difference and as the walls, although thick, were also un-insulated, it remained a cold house for as long as I lived there. There was no central heating with the Rayburn and kitchen being the focus of the house, part of the wall between the kitchen and the front room was removed leaving an archway into what became the dining room. An electric fire replaced the coal fire in here and, eventually, another electric fire replaced the open fireplace in the one remaining front room which was extended by moving the internal wall between this room and the llaethdy. Also, not surprisingly, the kitchen was modernised with a new sink and cupboards and the purchase of a refrigerator, while a freezer was put in the llaethdy. Dad also put a shower in this room as well as an outside toilet in the shed near the back door both of which were connected into the drain leading to the cesspit.

The other major change was to replace the top half of the gable end of the house, facing the vegetable garden. This was done in the early 1970s out of necessity as it was bowing outwards. At this time Lyndon had left university but I was still at Swansea so during the summer holidays we spent a few days removing the stones which made up the top half of the wall. We were also helped by Lyndon's friend and fellow player at Bridgend RFC, Doug Schick, the Canadian international who really loved the experience of staying in the Welsh countryside and the hospitality provided by mam, particularly her home cooking, as well as the physical challenge involved in the work. He was super polite and a pleasure to have at the house. The work was done under the supervision of Ieuan Harris, a local builder and friend of the family, who then replaced the stones with a standard concrete block cavity wall. We borrowed a tractor and trailer from a local farmer and parked it on the road beside the back steps. Once fully loaded we took the stones and dumped them onto the flat section in front of the quarry and thus the stones were returned to where they had probably originated.   The plan on the next page shows the layout of Brynislwyn and its location in relation to Wenvoe, Sychpant, Rhiwgoi and Rhoshill.

Key

R	Ruins		H	Rugby posts
Sw	Swing		W	Well
T	Toilet		S	Sheds
V	Vegetable patch		Ch	Chicken run
G	Garden		Ho	House
Cw	Cwm		Sp	Spring
Hb	Hay barn		Sg	Ysgubor
M	Milking sheds		C	Cooling house
Si	Silage barn		M	Milk stand
P	Pig sties		D	Dan Trip's field
Wf	Wenvoe's fields		' '	Gates

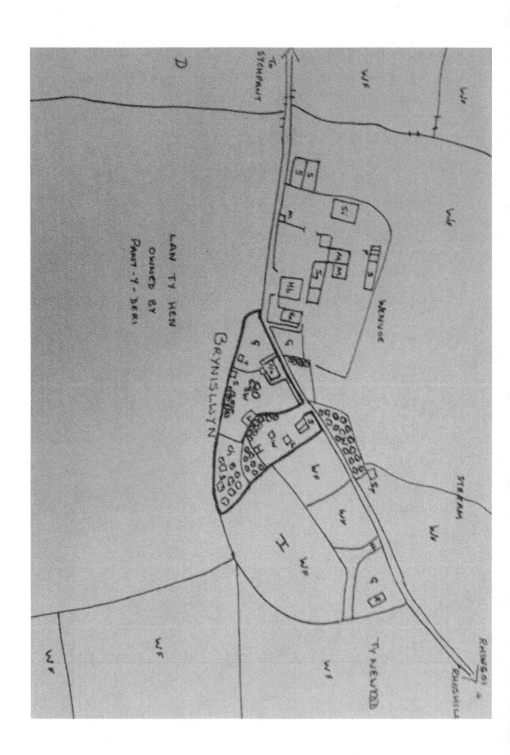

Outside the front there was a small lawn and hedge with a minor road running beyond and below the level of the hedge. It was half a mile down this road to Rhoshill and the main road to Cardigan and as you can imagine in the 1950s there wasn't much traffic. My **dadcu** (granddad) lived with us and I can remember that he had a car but we didn't get one until a few years later. The house was built on a piece of flat land which had been carved out of a slope. This meant that the top of the back garden was quite a bit higher than the road which ran below the front garden. I say garden but there was well over an acre of grounds, very little of it was flat but it was a great plot. Outside the back door there was a six foot wide dirt yard running the length of the house with a shed again dug out of the hill. Its zinc roof ran like an extension of the sloping back garden. When we were little we could walk straight off the grass onto the roof without danger of it giving way. Needless to say this was not encouraged. The back garden was accessible by about eight stone steps. The area had a mixture of shrubs, and grass with a couple of apple trees and a clothes line. There were some very impressive rhododendrons and another shed made out of stone walls and a zinc roof. The front half of this shed was used as a kennel for firstly corgis and later Pekingese. The rear half, separate from the front by a wooden wall was a disused pigsty which was mostly used to store the old wheelbarrow, some garden tools and rubbish. Continuing upwards you eventually came to a reasonably level area of grass, a small vegetable patch, a grassed area which contained another clothes line and finally a large area, the front half of which had little vegetation as it was used as a chicken run. The rear half of this area was covered in mature trees and the whole area was fenced off by a six foot high chicken wire fence.

There was another shed here, made entirely of zinc, which was the chicken coop. The chickens and eggs were obviously free range and were both a useful source of food. At one time we were also able to sell eggs. However it was always a constant battle with Mr Fox and after one such raid very few chickens survived and that was the final nail in the chickens' coffin. Most of the fence eventually became dilapidated and the area became a wild flower and grass area which together with the trees provided another fabulous play area. The fence was however maintained along the north boundary as the land fell away into a disused quarry which was covered by rhododendrons. From here the fabulous view of the hills, coast, town and villages to the north was even better than from the front windows and lawn (this view was partially blocked by trees). The quarry also looked down on another flat area, at the far end of which was the entrance to the property. The quarry provided us with another great play area. We could climb down amongst the trunks of the bushes (small trunks but small kids) to the flat area below. We could then run back up the path to the house, up the steps, up the garden, past the washing line and the vegetable plot and do it all over again. Even better and more dangerous was a game whereby we jumped from the edge of the quarry onto the rhododendron canopy and body surfed down to the bottom. As far as I can remember the worst injuries sustained were minor bumps and bruises and scratches.

If you approached the property from the road, there was a wide entrance, probably needed when the quarry was operational, and a large flat area made of compacted soil which had become pretty solid over the years; I suppose you could call this the drive. To the left was a grassed bank with access behind, and yes two more sheds. To the right parallel to the road there was a hedge containing a range of shrubs, and alongside there was a compacted soil path leading up towards the front lawn and around the east facing gable end of the house eventually linking with the area outside the back of the house. To the left of this path there was another bank containing more rhododendrons, several mature fir trees, which yielded masses of cones, and a grassed area which linked around to the bank behind the house. By stepping left off the path at numerous points you could access the top of the garden without having to go as far as the steps. At the far end of the drive, the flat land gave way to the lower edge of the quarry at the top edge of which you could see the chicken wire fence. A large part of the flat area below the quarry was overgrown for much of the year but contained a couple of productive hazel trees. Between these trees and the flat area were lots of wild and domestic shrubs including a mass of ferns plus a fresh water spring around which had been built a small well. Mam used to tell us about collecting water from here, for use in the house, when she was a girl. The quarry swept along to the left as you looked with your back to the road and on this slope the stone had been covered in soil and debris and overgrown with bushes. We had trodden all sorts of trails whereby we could make our way up the slope to emerge at the back of the tree area which lay beyond the chicken run. Dad had attached a rope to a tree at the top of this slope which we could use to help us climb up and down.

There were actually three sheds In this area, the first two, already mentioned being attached with their gable ends facing the road and the third, in front of and at ninety degrees to the other two was used for granddad's car. The first of the attached sheds was the largest. The lower half of the walls was made out of stone and soil, like the house, and the top half was a wooden structure topped by the inevitable zinc roof. The top of the wide walls either side served as shelves for all sorts of stuff. It had a big window at the pine end facing north overlooking the small grassed bank, the road and the view in the distance. There were two more windows on the side facing the drive and the other pine end contained two large wooden doors. When they were fully open you could drive a car into the shed. It had inside and outside lights which dad had rigged up from the house. It was basically a workshop, at the window end there was a large solid wooden work bench with a pair of vices, a three footed cast iron cobbler's anvil which he used to repair shoes plus a range of the usual hand tools. My dad was a magpie, he was reluctant to throw anything away, you never knew when it might prove useful and so he had a fair amount of stuff in the shed. Much of it was used as he was very good with his hands and would produce all sorts of

Heath Robinson gadgets. He might well have become and engineer or electrician had things turned out a little differently.

The two attached sheds viewed from the road with Brenda's children Rhys and Amy in their roller skates.

If you walked around the gable ends of the two sheds there was another banked area(on the extreme left of the picture) which contained a range of small trees and which had, in season, masses of snowdrops and wild primroses. At the back of the bank you could access a field through gaps we had made in the tree lined hedge. The area immediately alongside the shed between it and the bank and fields was about ten foot wide, reasonably flat and was used for what dad called **anibendod**. There is no exact translation in English but it basically means untidy rubbish. Dad maintained that every home needed such an area. The earliest use of the second shed that I can remember was partly as a potato store and partly as a coal store. The main-crop potatoes stored here were grown in a field at Wenvoe farm next door. They would provide the land to grow the potatoes, and sometimes broad beans and peas, in return for my father's free labour during harvest time. The store of spuds would be covered by a tarpaulin to keep out the light and cold and would last us through the winter and early spring. If we were lucky we wouldn't run out until next season's first earlies were ready. I can remember one year after a poor crop we had to buy in a load of potatoes. They were a really good size but had a blue dye on them. I found out later that this dye was an indication that they were meant for animal feed but we ate them without any lasting damage. Outside this shed there was a good sized open space where my father kept his log pile plus a metal stand used for sawing logs. We never had to buy any logs as there were a lot of old trees on our grounds and surrounding fields. Farmers would be grateful for any help in removing storm damaged trees; we could even borrow a tractor and trailer for the purpose.

The grounds contained one more area. Beyond the west facing pine end of the house was dad's pride and joy – the vegetable garden. This was quite a large triangular area. One side of the triangle had a hedge, more of a bank really, which ran parallel and about six foot above the road and this contained a gate and steps down to the road. My father had dug the steps into the bank and topped each one with blue flagstones and this served as a short cut to Wenvoe farm across the road where we got our milk. The top end of the garden had a hedge which separated it from a vast field (Lan Ty Hen) which bordered the southern boundary of our grounds and the third boundary ran from the kennel/pig sty down in front of the gable end of the house towards the road. One year after significant heavy rainfall the vegetable garden was flooded by water flowing off the big field known as Lan Ty Hen (literally translated as up new house) and half the soil was washed away and ended up as a dirty brown flow down the road. This prompted dad to build a ditch our side of the hedge bordering the field and to put a large pipe in it which drained the water out into the ditch running alongside the road and this solved the problem. Fortunately there was a good depth of good quality soil left and this was topped up over the next few years with manure and soil which could be 'foraged' from elsewhere locally. Next to the shed there was another gate which could access both the garden and the toilet which nestled in that angle of the triangle. The toilet entrance faced the hedge so you had to walk around it to get in. There was one solitary apple tree in the middle of the vegetable garden; otherwise it was divided into a series of vegetable patches. Here my father grew potatoes, onions, shallots, beetroot, cabbage, peas, broad beans and runner beans. There was a spot for rhubarb, mint, a senna bush and a few flowers. We were often given a dose of senna pods as apparently it was good for constipation. My brother and I would often pinch a saucer of sugar from the house, pick some rhubarb (also good for constipation!) and have a little picnic in one of our many dens. I suspect mam knew about this little crime but rarely let on! Mam and dad never seemed to bother much with the apple trees, windfalls would be used for making pies and chutney but I'm sure that the tree in the garden was an eating apple – possibly Golden Delicious. Some of the windfalls were fairly yellow and quite tasty but were usually small, I now realise that it was probably too much hassle to thin them out, in order to make sure that each apple left grew to a decent size. The grounds took quite a bit of tending and although it was done by dad and dadcu in the early 1950s, after dadcu died dad did it all on his own. Essential tools for the job were a scythe and sickle for cutting grass, weeds and lighter undergrowth and both long and short handled billhooks which made light work of hedges, shrubs, brambles and tougher weeds. An axe was also useful and a whetstone was essential to keep everything sharp.

In addition to the flood in the garden it was subjected to some damage when a few claves from Wenvoe somehow managed to get from the road up onto the bank and into the vegetable patch. It took a while but eventually we managed to remove the animals but not before they had caused quite a mess. Another time dad had an altercation with a swarm of wasps. There was a wasp's nest on the hedge of Wenvoe's property just opposite our vegetable garden and the wasps were a constant menace. Despite our efforts with jars of jam and water and our corgi Nip's attempts to bite them, they were a constant nuisance. Dad decided that there was only one thing to do and that was to kill them with smoke. So while Lyndon and I watched from our garden and John Allison, Sychpant, while sat on his bike, observed from the road, dad pushed a burning rag into the mouth of the nest. Unfortunately he was not aware that they had a back entrance and they came swarming after him while John was last seen haring down the road on his bike followed by a swarm of wasps. Fortunately he outran them by the time he got to the entrance to Wenvoe's fields at Ty Newydd, a few hundred yards down the road. Dad was not so lucky; he ran home and stripped his shirt off to expose a huge number of wasp stings on his chest and back. Fortunately he was not allergic and a wash in soapy water followed by liberal amounts of calamine lotion helped to reduce the pain. The presence of wasps seemed to be a regular thing at Brynislwyn and we just had to do our best to minimise their effects and learn to living with them.

It looks at first that we were quite well off with the large house, grounds, being partly self contained with food and having six sheds! In fact the property was rented at a peppercorn rent. Financially I know that my parents struggled but we were rich in quality of life. We never went without food. Fancy clothes (if even available at the time), didn't bother us, mam was good with her hands and could knit and sew effectively. Nor were we bothered about having lots of toys, far better were ones that dad made for us or we made ourselves. We were semi self sufficient and the richness of our surroundings made for a good life. My brother, sister and I had a really happy upbringing. I suspect that life was much harder for mam and dad but even for them life was easier than it was during their upbringing during the nineteen twenties and thirties. They were born just after the First World War and we were born just after the Second World War and of course, we have gone on to become baby boomers.

This is a picture of Brynislwyn and a large part of the grounds. The white triangular shape to the right edge of the pine end to the left of the greenhouse is the corrugated zinc roof of the shed situated at the back of the house. The vegetable garden can be seen to the right of the pine end with a greenhouse in the picture which did not exist in the 1950s. and at the top right hand corner there is a blackthorn tree where the toilet used to be. Near the top of the picture is the pine tree which had the swing attached with rhododendrons in front (and dad mowing the lawn!) and to the right and beyond the top the ground levels off towards the chicken run. At the top left hand corner there are a number of trees and here the ground gives way to the quarry with its coverage of rhododendrons. In front of Brynislwyn are the small lawn, hedge and road which slopes down in front of the path leading down to the entrance, drive and sheds. The roof of Wenvoe can be seen at the bottom of the picture with its front lawn and some soft fruit bushes. The narrow country road can be seen between the two houses.

Our Own Playground and Beyond

From my description it should be clear that the opportunities for play in the grounds were huge, so who needed lots of toys? One of our favourite games was Cowboys and Indians. We would cut old sacking to make costumes, bows and arrows were made out of the abundance of wood growing in our grounds or on nearby hedgerows, and bird feathers stuck in an old piece of elastic, or other material would serve as a head band. There were always old hats lying around but we did have toy guns and holsters. The guns fired caps so we thought they were very realistic. My brother being older and stronger than me mostly got to choose which character he wanted to be and more often than not he would be the cowboy, who of course in the films we had seen, always won. But I didn't mind, I liked being the Indian.

We could make catapults out of a Y shaped piece of wood and elastic. If we managed to get fairly thick elastic then this could be quite powerful and a bit dangerous of you fired stones. Usually we would fire them at targets like old tins and sometimes with little success we would fire them at pigeons as there were always plenty of them around. I once got into trouble for firing an arrow at an old lady called Annie Fach, who was walking down the road. The arrow didn't get that close but I still had a telling off and had to apologise to her. Sledges, for when we had snow, were made out of wood and old flat metal strips. These had previously been mattress supports on an old bed frame, (before we progressed to springs), and could be attached to wooden runners to make it go faster. Rubbing a bit of oil on them would make them even smoother and thus faster. We did some of the work ourselves but did need some help from dad.

He also showed us how to make a whistle. You needed a piece of wood about four to six inches long and about the thickness of a man's thumb, usually cut from a fresh hazel branch. It was necessary to use a pen knife to make a circular cut around the bark about an inch from one end. The piece of wood would than need to be soaked so that the bark would loosen from the wood and with a bit of twisting and persuasion would come away complete. This exposed fresh whitish wood, the top part of which would be cut away for an inch as far as the bark on the longer part of the wood thereby producing a flat surface, one inch long. At the end of this flat surface you would need to cut away downwards at an angle to remove a triangle of wood. Then slide the removed bark back over the wood, cut a semi circle out of the end of the bark and bob's your Uncle, you have a whistle. There would be a gap at the top inch of the wood between wood and bark into which you would blow and a hole in the bark for the air to come out as a whistle. Admittedly it was only one note but we could blow and suck to our hearts content.

I have already mentioned how we used to use the rhododendrons growing in the quarry but there were other patches of the shrub which provided mini woodlands and were therefore great for dens. We would clamber over and under branches and establish little rooms where we could put down old sacking or tarpaulins. These became useful places to imagine as mini kitchens and sitting rooms. We would use blocks of wood, old concrete blocks or general rubbish to furnish the rooms. These dens were also ideal for picnics of rhubarb and sugar or raw peas or sour apples with sugar, which were foraged from the vegetable garden 'illegally' or cakes, biscuits or sandwiches provided by mam. Sometimes the picnics would be sandwiches made out of leaves and mud. These leaves were also very handy for wiping your bottom because if you are busy playing it's often quite far to go all the way to the outside toilet. There were always plenty of little quiet corners which served as makeshift toilets. And it was always easy to bury the offending article. The rhododendrons provided a few of a host of places where you could play hide and seek, which could become a bit of a nightmare because of the number of options for hiding. They were especially useful when it was time to go in and get ready for a bath or bed. I don't think we were avid readers but we did occasionally sit in the dens with our books. But why would you want to read when there were so many places to explore, climb or run around?   Although the grounds and surrounding areas were extensive and we would play for hours there was never a problem with missing meals as mam had a large old school bell which she used to ring when it was time to eat.

The well at the end of the drive was built around a spring.   The well itself was covered with a solid piece of wood on top of which sat a large concrete block.   In front of the well there was a small pond area and most years this would have frog spawn, some of which we would collect and put in large jars and over the weeks watch the spawn develop into tadpoles and finally, frogs. If we were lucky we would see the occasional frog hopping around near the pond. The drive which ran alongside the workshop was a great flat area for playing football. One small problem was that as it approached the road it sloped down a little and we would often have to chase the ball into the road to prevent it running away down the road or over the hedge into the area the other side of the road. Mind you chasing the ball down the road or having to climb over the hedge to retrieve it was all part of the fun. It was less fun if the ball ended up in the undergrowth below the foot of the quarry as this inevitable contained brambles and stinging nettles. Fortunately, there were also plenty of dock leaves which, if rubbed into the nettle rash, provided some relief.

The problem of the undergrowth was even worse when we played cricket or rounders. Often it was just the two of us playing, but occasionally the farmer's daughter from next door, Mary, who was a year younger than me joined us and also the Allison children from Sychpant Farm further up the road came over regularly to play. This made both games more fun but it was always difficult to find the ball in the undergrowth. One way which we liked using was to get one of dad's old work coats, which were usually hanging in the shed, wrap it around us and dive into the undergrowth to flatten it. To be honest, I'm not sure if this helped much but it was great fun. Nettle rash on hands, arms and bare legs (we always wore short trousers especially in the summer) was pretty common. In winter it was surprising how many balls we would find when the plants had died back. This allowed us to restock ready for the next season. It was even more fun when mam and dad played with us. Mam was a real cheat when she was bowling; she would dummy throw and then when you were off balance roll the ball fast along the floor. This often worked to get us out among loud protests but fortunately the uneven compacted soil meant that the ball did not always end up where it was intended. She also used to do this with her grandchildren and now her great grand children!

Of course one activity which every child growing up in the countryside loved, I'm sure, was climbing trees and there were plenty of these in the grounds. There were several fir trees and we used to love collecting pine cones. We used to call them bings and they served as a good ingredient with mud, twigs, leaves and water in our homemade soup. Pine cones were also very good for burning like firewood. These trees were difficult to climb as they did not have many low branches but one of them, just above the dog 'kennel' more or less in the middle of the back garden had the perfect horizontal branch to hang a swing from. Two pieces of rope and a piece of wood and voila, you had your swing which provided hours of pleasure.

Brenda on the swing, the pine tree trunk is on the right with rhododendrons and the roof of the house in the background.

I was about five or six when I had my first bike. It was a three wheeler with no tyres on the metal rims, which just happened to be lying around in the shed. No matter, I loved that bike. Metal rims didn't matter much when riding around in the grounds but it was a bit bumpy and noisy on the road. It didn't have very good brakes either which again didn't matter in the grounds but could be a bit tricky on the road. Turing right out of the drive there was a two hundred yard stretch of road which was fairly flat so we could ride on this part fairly safely.   To the right there were fields which belonged to Wenvoe Farm next door. There were six in total, three of which were rarely used for crops but I suppose they were useful for cattle grazing but usually seemed overgrown with weeds.

The layout of our grounds alongside these fields allowed easy access to a huge area for play and exploration. We would use these fields to walk on, run on for foraging and just generally explore. Three of the fields were quite large and were used for hay or wheat and straw production. One of these which ran down towards the road was quite steep and ideal for winter sledging on snow or summer sledging once the hay or wheat had been harvested. Access to these fields was through a gate leading to a short farm track which led to the big steep field. The other fields were accessed off this track. The fields were collectively known as Ty Newydd (New House). This was because to the left of the track there was a ruin of an old house (Ty Newydd which was obviously new when it was first built!) together with a small garden which had a damson tree growing amongst the neglected undergrowth. This provided a handy source of fruit for jam making.   Hedges provided ample blackberries for **clampofers** and if we were lucky, wild strawberries which we would collect and slide onto a long piece of grass until it was full enough to provide a decent portion for immediate consumption. Opposite the house and to the right of the track was a fairly large flat area which looked as it had been dug out of the bank and resembled a small quarry. I suspect that this is where many of the stones used to build the house had come from.   The derelict house, garden and immediate surrounds was a favourite place for playing firstly by myself, Lyndon and our friends and later Brenda and her friends.

As already mentioned, a huge field ran alongside the south side of our grounds and so we were able to explore this area as well. Dad had in fact put in a little stile from our back garden into the field thereby giving us easy access although it did involve some jumping off the hedge into the field and some climbing to get back out into our garden. This was the field known as Lan Ty Hen. This large field always seemed to be full of wheat or corn and watching harvest time was a real treat. One year a friend from school, who was a year older than Lyndon was in the field and he climbed over the style to join us in our garden, and for some reason I hit him with a hammer! More recently an underground reservoir has been built at the top of this field accessed by a private road built through Wenvoe's fields at Ty Newydd.

My brother also had a three wheeler but he had tyres! If the brakes didn't work too well we could turn right at the end of the flat bit of road into the wide opening which led to the gate to Ty Newydd. There was a slight incline towards the gate and this was quite effective in slowing us down. Slightly to the right of the road and left of the gate there was a telegraph pole which had a thick wire running at about a sixty degree angle from the top and was anchored into the ground. This triangle proved irresistible and we would aim our bikes between the pole and wire. The grass under the pole and beyond would serve as a good brake. If you misjudged you could hit the right handlebar against the wire which would stop the bike dead while you continued in a forward direction. Fortunately the grass and undergrowth provided a soft landing and didn't contain too many nettles and brambles. From here the road became quite steep for almost half a mile down towards the main road. We were discouraged from going down this far but it didn't always stop us. I can remember once going too fast (even without tyres), losing control and crashing. I had a nasty bruise on the back of my head as well as the expected cuts and grazes on my arms and knees. Needless to say travel down this hill was banned for some time but my parents couldn't police us all the time.

****

Half way down this hill was a small cottage called Fern Cottage but which was known locally as Rhiwgoi (apparently its original name). This was the home of the Edwards family our near neighbours. There was Jimmy, Mair and three boys, Tony who was four years younger than me, David, who was two years younger than Tony was the same age as my sister and the youngest, Peter was born in 1964, so was quite a bit younger than the rest of us. The two families were good friends as well as being immediate neighbours. Jimmy was a local boy from Blaenffos, one of six children. Before doing national service he had started as a builder/stonemason's apprentice but afterwards he worked at Cardigan Railway Station as a mechanic. He would travel to work on his motor bike and often Tony and David would run down to Rhoshill to meet him and they would have a ride home, Tony on the back and David on the petrol tank. When the railway closed he worked with the Water Board, working up to area manager well before he retired. Jimmy was very skilful and often helped local families, including us, with various building related jobs, often for free much to the annoyance of his wife Mair. We would often play with the Tony and David and we would walk together (and sometimes run) to catch the bus to school.

Mair was a North Wales girl and also one of six children. She came to the area to work on a farm and her and Jimmy moved into Rhiwgoi soon after they were married. Jimmy soon started renovating the cottage and he seemed to be at it for years. On one side it had vehicular access to the rear of the grounds where two sheds were located. One of these was used for chickens and over the years they also kept pigs, calves, and bred dogs. For a few years they also bred turkeys for sale at Christmas and one year, according to Tony, one of these turkeys grew to over forty pounds. To the other side of the cottage there was a vegetable garden and both Jimmy and Mair were keen gardeners. Mair used to sell vegetables at the roadside and even sold produce to the mobile shop that used to call weekly. My mother tells the story of an incident which happened at Rhiwgoi before the Edwardes move in. John Bathhouse, a local character who lived a mile or so past our house was walking home one night from the local pub at Rhoshill and it was snowing heavily. As he walked past Rhiwgoi he could see the elderly couple who lived there, sat at the table eating cawl (traditional Welsh soup), they hadn't seen him so he decided to throw a snowball at the window. Unfortunately, either because the snowball was hard or it contained a stone, it broke the window and landed in their cawl. Mam thought this was very amusing but I don't expect that the inhabitants of Rhiwgoi agreed with her.

****

At the bottom of the hill, which ran past Rhiwgoi, the road became flat again and about a hundred yards further on it ended at a cross roads. Straight across there was a minor road running down to the nearest village Cilgerran, which was about two miles away. To the left the main road, the A478, ran northwards and downwards towards Cardigan and to the right southwards and upwards towards other villages including Blaenffos and Crymmych, and onwards towards the Preseli Hills and eventually to the A48 which led to Carmarthen and Haverfordwest. It was at this crossroads that the little hamlet called Rhoshill was located and which contained a small shop with a post office, a public house, a blacksmith, five houses and a red telephone kiosk. Although describing itself as a shop, the shelves as far as I can remember, seemed rather empty. There seemed to be plenty of Persil and Vim and we could buy Wagon Wheels but not much else. We did get a daily paper from here however and the post office was handy. The business was run by Bella Shop who lived with and was occasionally helped by her sister called Annie Fach and she was indeed very small! I suppose that, being so close to the end of the war, stuff was still difficult to get hold of but it seems that Bella operated her own rationing system. Mam told me a story about someone going into the shop and asking for matches but Bella said she didn't have any. A niece of hers, who was staying with her, apparently pointed out that there were plenty of matches under the counter. Bella was selective about who she served it seems. Bella and Annie were both spinsters and when the shop closed in the mid to late 1950s they continued to live in the house for several more years. We children could be quite unkind to Annie when she walked up the road with her stick, I've already mention the bow and arrow incident, we would also call her names and jump out of bushes to frighten her, she would wave her stick at us and walk on.

The pub called the Foundry Arms was on the road down to Cilgerran. It was run by a chap we knew as Norman Foundry (surname Wright) and his wife Sally. As the building also housed the Wright family, the bar was fairly small but big enough to accommodate its local clientele. It had a blue flagstone floor, tables and chairs and several wooden settles. Dad would often disappear to the Foundry for a few hours on a Saturday evening but he wasn't really much of a drinker, although he did like his brandy and kept his stash hidden in the airing cupboard.

The blacksmith, or gof in Welsh, was owned and run by Evan Owens, known locally as Evan Gof or Ianto Gof, with the help of my cousin Leslie who had both helped dad with our bathroom. It was on the Cardigan road and wasn't particularly big, a single storey building with the fire hearth and large bellows at its centre with an anvil and a range of tools but it was a hive of activity, heat and noise. Evan wore a large leather apron and goggles as he went about his work. He was an excellent craftsman who could produce and repair a range of metal products like gates, railings, tools, agricultural implements and machinery, the metal parts of carriage wheels as well as making and fitting horseshoes and he made works of art out of wrought iron. He could of course also turn his hand to plumbing if required. He continued in business until about 1970 when he and his wife emigrated to Calcutta to join their daughter whose husband was from India and had previously worked as a doctor in South Wales. The site was taken over by someone called Hodges who used to make oil central heating tanks and Tony Rhiwgoi used to have a Saturday job there. Today the site is occupied by a house and the large workshop of an engineering company which produces pumping equipment for a whole range of uses.

Across the main road from the post office there was a large square house – the poshest house in the village – occupied by a single lady who may have been widowed. Later Arthur James of Close Farm (where I worked one summer) and his wife Verona moved in when they retired. Between this house and the foundry Arms was a small cottage where various families lived for short periods. In the 1960s the Potts family lived there including Oliver who was a year younger than me. There was a short terrace of three houses on the right going up Windy Hill from the junction. In the first on the corner lived Vivian Thomas and his two sisters (whose names I think were Gladys and Maggie) who were very nice and would regularly chat to us on our way home from school. They had a long vegetable garden which ran parallel to the lane going up to Brynislwyn. At the end of the garden, in the spring there was a wonderful variety of daffodils. The middle house was occupied by Evan Owen the blacksmith and his wife and daughter and Jean remembers visiting them once and seeing their daughter (who was grown up and had left home) dressed in a sari which was probably quite unusual in West Wales at the time. The end house was occupied by Ellis and Gladys Nicholas. Ellis worked on the roads and Gladys worked at Close Farm. We knew them quite well and I can remember when visiting them they had a fairly aggressive Pekingese dog, whose bark was worse than his bite. The aggression was a bit of a surprise as our Pekingese were pretty quiet and docile. Today the hamlet has grown to more than double its former size but apart from the engineering works it is made up entirely of houses.

A little further down the road toward Cardigan lived brother and sister, Dan and Olwen Trip, this being the name of the farm not their surname. Dan owned land near Rhiwgoi and he also had a field on the road to Sychpant. In addition to running a farm Dan was an agent for stock feed, particularly for pigs, and would supply most of the local farmers. We knew them quite well and when we were older used to help out during hay harvest. The opposite way towards Crymmych, at the top of Windy Hill lived an Italian named Carlo

Frishgoni. He worked on this farm when he was a prisoner of war and decided to settle in this country rather than go back to Italy. When the owner of Windy Hill Farm died, as he had no family of his own, he left the farm to Carlo who later brought his wife and daughter over from Italy and his family continued to farm Windy Hill for many decades. His land bordered Wenvoe's fields on one side of the road. There was a path which ran behind his farm into Wenvoe's fields which we would often use as a short cut during our explorations and sometimes when we went to primary school as we caught the bus almost opposite the entrance to the farm. Also at this junction to Boncath was a bungalow called Gerallt. In 1954 the Payne family moved in and they had three children including Jennifer who became Jean Allison's best friend.

****

Turning left up the road from our drive was, if we went by bike, a safer option than going down the hill to the main road and there was more to explore along the many country lanes, fields and woods. There was firstly a hill which ran past Wenvoe, before levelling out for about a mile, with fields on both sides, before coming to another farm, Sychpant, the home of the Allison family. We would sometimes continue beyond Sychpant for another half mile or so, past a few houses and farms, as off this road there was a field which gave access to the ruins of an old house whose garden in early spring was full of daffodils. We had no idea who owned it but going home with a few bunches of daffodils certainly earned brownie points with mam. Along this road there was one section of hedge on which grew small purple sweet berries which we knew as wind berries - further foraging bounty. This road went from Rhoshill to link with the A487 Cardigan to Fishguard road. About a mile along from that junction was the village of Eglwyswrw which a few years ago was said to be the wettest place in the UK after ninety consecutive days of recorded rainfall.

When I was a bit older I got my first two wheeler bike which was bought second hand from my uncle for ten shillings (fifty pence in new money). The bike had belonged to my female cousin. It was a girl's bike, the type typically seen in period dramas on television. It was black with ninety degree handlebars and a basket on the front (which I soon ditched) and no gears but it did have tyres! Despite it being a girl's bike I loved it. It didn't have a bar across the top which meant I could get on and off easily as I was too small to get easily onto a boy's bike. It also had wide tyres which proved to be great on rough terrain and fields – perhaps an early version of a mountain bike! It was also handy for the bike races at various local village sports events which were held in farmers' fields and popular in the summer. Having a two wheeler bike also meant we could explore a little further afield. Luckily the country roads, although narrow, were pretty quiet. They were maintained by 'the roadman' who regularly cut the hedges and cleared the ditches along all the narrow lanes. One of these was Ellis Nicholas from Rhoshill whom I have already mentioned. With the simplest of tools; a sickle, hook, scythe and hay fork they would, after the flush of summer growth and flowering, cut back the roadside hedges and verges, piling their cuttings into regular heaps which would then be collected by another man in a lorry. In the winter these men were kept busy clearing and maintaining the ditches and drains using mostly no more than a long handled spade. They had ruddy complexions working through all weathers and wearing a waterproof cape if it rained. The narrow single road surfaces were sealed by tarmac but often the central strip would sprout grass and weeds; the narrower and less used the road, the more growth there was. Every few years a noisy, smoky and smelly coal fired traction engine and roller would come along to re-tar and re-seal the roads. I suppose the job was not much different to what they do now it's just that the machinery was a bit older and usually coal driven and it was all more labour intensive.

My Dad the Entrepreneur, Mam, Dadcu and Islwyn

Dad was born and grew up on a small holding near a village called Tegryn. He was the youngest of seven with two brothers and four sisters. Life growing up for him was extremely tough; he was educated at the local school until he left at fourteen to become a farm hand. Having no form of transport and a long working day, for his first job he lived in at a farm a few miles from where he was brought up. The farm owner and his wife had no children of their own so he was treated as if he was theirs. His life involved plenty of food, a long hard working day and lots of kindness. He started work in 1936 and being a key worker he was not required to enlist during the Second World War. As his employer had an important job with the Ministry of Agriculture, dad ended up more or less running the farm on his own. He worked at a few other farms before his final one which was called Pantyderi farm and mansion. There were quite a few of these mansions spread around the area and each one had a large parcel of land. Pantyderi's land actually bordered our garden and while it was about a mile away across the fields, the shortest route was two to three miles via the country lanes.

My dad was short and stocky, five foot five with a forty two inch chest. He was very fast, strong and hard working. I remember we used to have sprint races with him in the field next to the chicken run and we were quite old before we managed to beat him. When he filled the corn sacks on the combine harvester at Pant-y-Deri the other farm hands would complain that he filled them too full as they struggled to handle them. As he had thick black hair and a well tanned skin, people used to tease him that he must have some Mediterranean blood in him. During his early years working and while he was courting he had a motor bike and apparently was not averse to roaring around the local villages. He would often take my mother's younger brother Islwyn on the back and they were a right pair of tearaways, whenever they saw the local bobby Islwyn would put his hands behind him to cover the number plate, but I would be very surprised if the policeman didn't know who it was. He would often race on the road between Boncath and New Chapel and he told me a story once of when a rival of his had a brand new shinny Japanese bike and challenged dad to a race, but dad still won.

When he got married in 1948 he moved in with my mam's family and joined her father working as a rabbit trapper. For this work they had a small pony (which I had always thought was a big horse) and a trap/cart, which they made themselves, and a set of rabbit traps. A lot of his work centred on Pantyderi because they had so much land but that employment came to an abrupt end when myxomatosis was introduced into the UK in 1953 which wiped out the rabbit population. I'm pretty sure that he kept the pony for a little longer as I can certainly remember him riding it in the fields. I once remember him going hell for leather with my brother on his lap before turning a little too sharply resulting in both taking a heavy fall; fortunately, nothing was broken. He then had a few years employed by the Water Board before enrolling as a fire officer for the Ministry of Defence at the local rocket testing station in Aberporth and he worked there for thirty years until he retired in 1986. He would work shifts - mornings, days, afternoons and nights - and a minibus would come to collect him and bring him home, although occasionally he would take his own car. In the whole time he was there he didn't have to deal with one serious incident but a fire crew had to be available every time the bloodhound missiles were tested and whenever an aeroplane landed. In his sixties he still had to prove his fitness with regular tests which included the fireman's lift.

During these years at Brynislwyn his entrepreneurial skills led him to breed chickens, dogs and pigs as well as selling cabbage plants to his work colleagues. He would visit a local farm which had fields of young cabbage plants, he and the farmer would pick the plants in bunches of twenty five or fifty and he would then take a boot full to sell at his workplace where he was known as Tom Cabbage. He would also grow these plants in the vegetable garden and when I was older I would go with him to pick and collect the young plants and a little later on my own. The baby cabbage plants would be planted in fields of five or six acres and the farmer would send me to the field to pick the number I wanted and then it was just a case of carefully pulling them out of the ground so as not to damage the roots too much and counting them into bunches of twenty five or fifty (with one or two extra for luck) and tying the bunches with pieces of string. He bought baby chicks from a local supplier (gorgeous little bright yellow fluffy things) and placed them in a large heated metal contraption, a bit like a propagator, for a few weeks. This was important as baby chicks need quite a bit of heat until they have developed their full coat of feathers at about a month old. They were then transferred to the chicken coop until they were large enough to venture out into the chicken run.

The female dogs and pigs gave birth at home and once ready dad would have no problem selling them. The pigs would be taken by Allison Sychpant, who had his own cattle truck, to a market in Hereford, for sale and slaughter. Sometimes dad would go with him and return with lots of fresh vegetables and other goodies. Apparently David Rhiwgoi also went with Allison once (to accompany their pigs I expect) but was a bit shocked by the whole experience when he realised what was to happen to them. We had a male Corgi called Nip as well which obviously had one use but otherwise was a real pain. He once returned from his wanderings and a few days later we had a visit from an irate neighbour complaining that our corgi had spoilt the pedigree of his female dog – I don't remember which breed. Otherwise Nip would spend his time barking, jumping and snapping to try and kill wasps in his mouth and chasing the few cars and cycles which went past our house. When we had a car and dad had been out somewhere, he had an uncanny ability to meet the car at Rhoshill and would run home barking at the car all the way. It's a miracle he never got run over as he seemed to have a thing for car tyres.

When the Corgis became too old to breed and died, dad replaced them with Pekingese. We started with one female pup. (Toots) and when she produced her first litter he kept one of them (named Dot) so that we effectively had two pets each of which would regularly produce litters which were then sold. At that time Pekingese could be sold for quite a good price. When Toots and Dot became quite old they were given away to two elderly couples that dad knew, so we were happy that they both had good homes. Once they were gone dad didn't breed any more dogs. He also fancied himself as a bit of a barber. Well actually this involved cutting our hair, he had hair clippers and a scissors and short back and sides was the order of the day. Once while cutting Lyndon's hair he accidentally cut his ear and anyone who has had a cut ear will know that it bleeds profusely. There was blood everywhere but fortunately there were also spiders everywhere so we had enough cobwebs and they are great at stemming the flow of blood; well it worked on my brother's ear anyway.

****

Mam was a typical Welsh housewife. Short, slim and hard working, she would make sure that there was always food on the table, that we had clean clothes, that the house was kept in good order, that her children were polite and well behaved (failed!) as well as doing a fair share of looking after the animals. Friday would be washing day and Monday would be cleaning day.

Looking back it was amazing to think how self sufficient we were in terms of food production. As well as using fresh vegetables from the garden, mam would do a great deal of home baking using fruit from the garden and surrounding countryside as well as producing various home-made drinks. Elderflower and elderberry wines were produced every year as well as lemonade and elderflower champagne which was a non alcoholic fizzy drink. It's amazing what a large earthenware pot, fruit, water and yeast can produce. Jams and chutneys would use up any glut or damaged fruit and vegetables. As already mentioned we would love to go foraging for many of the items used. Eggs and milk were plentiful so half the ingredients needed for a range of cakes were easily available. Welsh cakes and pancakes were great favourites and were regularly produced and she would also quite often make her own bread. This time the earthenware pot, covered in a tea towel would be used to hold the dough and be placed next to the fire to slowly rise before being kneaded, shaped into the bread and baked in the oven. It was hard to know which was nicest, freshly baked bread or freshly cooked blackberry **clampofer**. In season certain vegetables would be plentiful and we used to enjoy shelling (and eating) peas. The most plentiful crop was probably runner beans and I we used to regularly have a plateful of these beans, topped with butter, for lunch. I used to love them, and still do although Lyndon and Brenda weren't quite as enthusiastic.

Mam would help out on the farm next door during harvest time, helping to prepare and bring food and hot tea to the fields so that the harvesting labour had a break without having to move out of the fields. Hot tea with milk and sugar out of a big metal jug and poured into proper cups was always welcome, tasted really good and was an excellent thirst quencher even in hot weather. She was also particularly good with flowers and had a range of flowering shrubs and pots of flowers in the garden that backed onto the rear of the house. Anything would do for pots from old toilets to a variety of metal containers like old watering cans and even an old bathtub.

She was born in the Rhondda and her father was a miner, but he moved for health reasons with his family to the countryside near the village of Boncath and she went to the local school in Blaenffos. She was the youngest of four children with three older brothers, Jim, Trevor and Islwyn. Like dad she left school at fourteen and although probably bright enough she was not considered for grammar school as at that time you had to pay and her parents were poor with the added disadvantage that she was a girl. Her first job was as a member of the housekeeping staff at a local mansion, Ffynone, which was just outside Boncath.

Ffynone House, a Grade I listed Georgian mansion lies in the centre of Ffynone Estate and is surrounded by about thirty acres of parkland. The name comes from the Welsh **ffynnonau** meaning wells because of the abundance of wells in the area. It was designed by the famous architect John Nash who is well known for the terraces that surround Regents Park in London. It was first built in 1799 and in 1907 the house and gardens were remodelled and redesigned by the architect and garden designer Indigo Thomas. This is one of many such buildings and estates dotted around this part of North Pembrokeshire. During the Second World War the mansion became a rehabilitation centre for injured servicemen and mam trained as an auxiliary nurse and joined the WRVS. When her mother died she had to give up her job and move in with her dad and her younger brother so she could look after them. This was soon after the war but before she got married.

As we got older she worked part-time at her brother Islwyn's pub in Cardigan doing anything required to help keep it running but her speciality was her roast dinners cooked on a Monday for the farmers who attended the local livestock market. After a good day at the market the beer and spirits flowed pretty freely and a fine roast dinner helped things along. She continued to help after her brother died in 1974 as the new owners could see her value to the business. She also continued her voluntary work for the Welsh version of WRVS and later for the Welsh version of the Women's Institute, **Merched Y Wawr**. I remember when she was about eighty, still going to volunteer at a day centre helping with food for what she called the 'old people', most of whom were younger than her!

****

Dadcu is Welsh for granddad. As already mentioned he lived with us in the early 1950s or I suppose I should say that we lived with him as it was his family home. Mam had moved in when her mother died and dad moved in when they got married. He had the smallest of the bedrooms upstairs which he seemed quite happy with. He did not live long enough to enjoy the luxury of an indoor bathroom. I don't remember a lot about him but what I do remember is to do with lots of fun which I suppose is only normal with grandparents. **Dadcu** worked on the roads with the local council before his rabbit trapping days and he died not long after myxomatosis wiped out his rabbit trapping business. He had his own car which we loved to play in and go for rides up the road. He would sometimes let us sit in his lap to steer the car.

He always seemed kind and jovial and a favourite trick of his when he broke wind was to send us running after it through the house and of course we fell for it every time or maybe we just played along. Apparently once I had broken a window pane with a hammer and he gave me the hammer and asked me to show him how I had done it. So I did. How was I to know that he didn't want me to actually hit the window? Dad couldn't get too cross with me as I was only (for once) doing what I was told!

Dadcu stood at the back of the house in the early 1950s

Mam's brother, Islwyn, had moved out and got married before my mam and dad married and dad moved into Brynislwyn. Islwyn moved to Cardigan as he worked at the railway station. He lived in a small terraced house on Finch Square which was to the east of the town. The square was a large area and served as a major bus stop for the town, with room for four or five busses at the same time. It was lined on one side by the terraced houses and a few shops and opposite was a church and graveyard. The local hospital was just around the corner and it was a short walk to the main shopping street and cinema, so an ideal spot for what was more or less an outdoor bus station. This was before the Beeching Cuts of the 1960s and when the cuts were implemented Islwyn became landlord of The Eagle Inn public house situated near the river on the south side of the old bridge. In fact one of the town's main riverside quays was accessed through a small road behind the public house and the buildings and warehouses were still active in the 1950s and 1960s and even have limited use today. Both the livestock market and railway station were situated on Station Road, on the south side of the town just opposite the Eagle Inn so an easy walk for the thirsty farmers after a successful sale. The market site was owned and run by J J Morris probably the most well know auctioneer and estate agent in the area. They also ran markets in Crymmych, Newcastle Emlyn and Whitland amongst others.

After a few years Islwyn and his wife parted and this is when my mother started working with him. He was a real character and being a publican really suited his jovial personality. He was in his element amongst the farmers on mart day. In the late 1960s and beyond I would often help him out and one piece of advice he gave, that I will always remember, is that it was better for business if you listen to the person ordering and paying for the drinks and not to the ones he's buying them for. After a good day at the auctions the farmers would always be free spending and would often buy a round without the knowledge of the recipients. Islwyn also dabbled in a bit of bed and breakfast as he had half a dozen bedrooms and whenever I could,

I would go down early in the morning to cook breakfast which was usually a full Welsh. On one visit to help in the bar and with a bit of cleaning I took my future wife Joanne so I could introduce them. He decided that she had to sit on a stool at one end of the bar while he chatted to her in between serving customers. He asked her what her favourite drink was and she told him Bacardi and coke, she told me later that she had to drink it very slowly because as soon as her glass was empty he would refill it. My stag do was held at his pub with my brother, father and a few of my and my brother's friends. It should have been good business for him but I'm not sure how much profit he made that evening!

His pub., The Eagle Inn was at the junction of the main road and of the road from St Dogmaels (Llandudoch in Welsh) where the local policeman called Jones Llandudoch was based. A couple of miles south of Cardigan in Pen-y-bryn the pub, The Pen-y-bryn Arms, was run by Islwyn's friend Dai Pen-y-bryn. One night Islwyn (for once – probably a quiet night with few customers) had shut the Eagle pretty soon after closing time and he noticed Jones Llandudoch go past the window on his motorbike so he called Dai on the phone. It took a few minutes before Dai answered (he must have been quite busy because Islwyn could hear a lot of noise in the background) and when he put the phone down he shouted at his customers to drink up as Islwyn Eagle had been on the phone to say that Jones Llandudoch was on his way – just as the bobby came in through the door. Severe warnings all round were the order of the day (or the night!). One summer it was particularly warm and Islwyn didn't have any short sleeved shirts so he decided to create a couple of his own with a pair of scissors. The sleeves ended up being different lengths and ragged but he didn't mind, he thought it was a great joke. At least it gave the customers something to talk about.

Islwyn would be a regular visitor to our house for Sunday lunch, although he would invariably be late as he would always find a local watering hole for a drink before lunch. I could never figure out why he was so keen on the home made elderflower wine, after all we were sometimes given this with hot water, if we had a cold, and we thought it was foul. But he was great fun and would always slip us some loose change. Sadly Islwyn died in 1974 at the age of fifty two and we were all very sad to see him go. He was a real character and spoilt us rotten; particularly Brenda and I would have loved to see what he would have made of our daughters. Meanwhile mam and dad continued to live in Brynislwyn long into their retirement until in 2008 at the ages of eighty-five and eighty-six they realised that the property was becoming too much to manage and moved into a bungalow in Pen-y-bryn which had previously been occupied by dad's brother and wife. Dad had tried out getting some help from friends with some of the tasks at Brynislwyn but 'they didn't do it properly'. The move allowed dad to continue with a much smaller vegetable garden and mam to work on her beloved flowers. Dad was ninety six before he stopped digging some of the small beds in the garden, although for a couple of years he had been getting someone in to dig over the large patch where he grew potatoes, runner beans and broad beans – although 'they didn't do it properly'!

The **Cwm**, Wenvoe and Sychpant

The English for **cwm** is valley and what we called the **cwm** could, at a push, be called a small valley. It had a small spring running down to a stream and continuing along the edge of a field. There were two gentle slopes either side of the stream, one being the edge of a field and the other being the **cwm**. The **cwm** started opposite the entry to our drive and continued for about two hundred yards parallel to the road that led to Rhoshill. The road was bordered by a low stone wall over which you could see the **cwm** fall away towards the stream. A range of trees grew on the slope of the **cwm** and in spring flowers carpeted large areas of the ground. I suppose it was basically a small wooded area which sloped down to a small stream.

There were also two or three old car wrecks nestling amongst the trees which had been abandoned and pushed over the low wall. We could access the **cwm** in several ways, some easy and some difficult but the trees, slopes, tracks and cars provided a perfect play area. The stream was great for damming with clods of earth and stones, which allowed us to create pools for paddling in, with or without wellington boots. In fact the water was so clean and pure that a well had been built around the spring and a pump added and this provided all the water that Wenvoe Farm needed and being a working dairy farm that was quite a lot. The stream continued northwards along the contours of the land and gradually became bigger until it eventually ran into the Teifi near Cilgerran. You could exit the **cwm** into the fields which lay on both sides of the stream. These provided further scope for exploration and foraging for blackberries, strawberries and in the build up to Christmas, holly.

****

The **cwm** and fields belonged to Wenvoe which was a fairly typical eighty acre mixed farm with dairy cattle and crop growing to feed the animals. A few pigs were reared there too. We probably spent as much of our time on the farm as we did at home. It was run by two brothers, Brynley and Jack Richards. They had been left the farm by their father Howell who had retired to one of four houses near Glanpwllafon Farm situated just north of Pen-y-bryn on the road to Cardigan. We would see Howell most years during harvest time. He was short, thin, and hunched over a walking stick and always seemed to have loose mints in his pocket. He would always offer us one and we didn't like to refuse despite the dubious colour compared with the original white. He also introduced Lyndon and I to smoking by letting each of us have half a cigarette each. Well I say introduced, we both coughed wildly and were violently sick, which put us off smoking for life. Perhaps that was the plan.

Brynley was fairly tall, mind you everyone looked tall alongside our family, and he was wiry and was a really cheerful character, full of fun. He was married to Peggy and they had two children, Mary, who was a year younger than me, and Glyndwr. As he was a year younger than my sister, he didn't figure much in our lives in the 1950s. Mary liked to hang around with us and wanted to join in but we weren't always keen, I mean she was younger and a girl! Jack was shorter than Brynley, a little broader with a round ruddy face. I think that he suffered from a respiratory problem called Farmer's Lung caused by overexposure to dust from hay and other crops and died relatively young. Peggy was a typical farmer's wife, kind, cheerful, down to earth, hard working with always plenty of food on the table and a cup of tea always on offer. She was probably the brains and driving force behind the operation. The family were regular chapel goers and the local preacher would often go to Wenvoe for Sunday dinner after the morning service and on most Sundays, after a hearty dinner, Brynley and the preacher could be found fast asleep on the couch in the front room.

The farmhouse wasn't that different in age and layout to our house. It had four rooms downstairs and four bedrooms upstairs. As far as I can remember the kitchen always had a Rayburn stove and they had an indoor bathroom before us. They also had a television and a telephone. We used to spend quite a bit of time in their kitchen and I remember Brynley having, what I thought, was an amazing filing system for bills. He used a piece of wire which he bent into a swan shape and he stuck each piece of paper over the wire so that during the year, the pile would grow in size. He had one of these for each year and he would hang them in a cupboard in the kitchen. He had the knack of being able to look up and find any bill with ease.

He also used to charge the battery for the electric fence in the kitchen. The electric fence is a simple contraption, a long piece of wire threaded through thin metal poles which are stuck in the ground and strung along the length of a field of grass of other fodder crop. This allows the cattle to graze as far as the boundary provide by the fence but if they touch it they get a small electric shock. They soon learn where the boundary is. Anyway this one time he was charging the battery and it still had a wire attached to it. He asked me to shake his hand, which I did and then nearly jumped out of my skin. He was holding the wire in one hand and transferred the electric shock through his other hand to me. Needless to say, I learned fast like the cattle and didn't fall for that one again. Apparently Brynley would also take an old hen which had stopped laying (in Welsh we would call her a 'iar glwc') and hang her from the clothes line in order to encourage her to lay. My dad told me recently that it made no difference and that he probably did it just to mess around to entertain the kids.

The back of the house was accessed either through a gate from the farmyard or at the opposite end down some steps from the road. There was an enclosed yard of large slate slabs (later concreted over) from which you could enter the house through the back door. Facing the back of the house on the other side of the yard was a coal house, outside toilet (which flushed) and workshop, which was smaller and a lot more crowded than our shed. The rest of the yard was bordered by a wall on top of which sat a couple of oil tanks with the hay barn immediately beyond them. The front of the house faced a small neat lawned and flowered garden. The lawned area contained a range of shrubs and was accessed from the road, via a pedestrian gate and was split by a path running parallel to the house, past the front door to another gate which led into the farmyard and the back of the house. To the right of the lawned area was a good sized vegetable plot with soft fruit bushes, particularly gooseberries and blackcurrants. Beyond the bottom hedge of the garden was a large pond and then the **cwm**.

The farm's day revolved around milking which happened twice a day, every day come rain or shine. The day would start early with a light meal called **bara te** - bread and tea served in a soup bowl. Often no alarm clock was needed as Brynley would wake to the sound of the transport driving up to collect dad to start the early shift at Aberporth. Then the sheep dog would be sent off to round up the cows ready for milking. The cows didn't need much encouragement to line up near the cowshed ready for their feed and to produce the goods. There were in fact two cowsheds, the second smaller and more modern than the main one. The cows would troop in and find a vacant berth, and they would be tethered by a large metal collar which would be clicked shut around their necks. The clasp was a long oval shape which gave the cows plenty of room to move their heads up and down while feeding from the trough but was narrow enough to prevent them from getting their head out and thereby reversing out of their berth. You could guarantee that each cow would empty its bowels before starting which made the cowshed pretty mucky but I suppose that was better than doing it once the milking machine was attached. Beyond the row of troughs there was a walkway leading to the ysgubor and from which cattle feed could be placed in the troughs. Brynley used to lift us onto a high window sill where we would sit counting the milk churn labels while also taking in all the activity.

The first job was to wash the udders and then attach the milking machine cups to the teats. These machines were cone shaped stainless steel buckets, wider at the bottom on top of which sat a contraption called a pulsator. This had two airlines or tubes and one milk tube. One airline and milk tube were attached to the claw which was made up of four teat cups which fitted over the cow's teats. The other airline was attached to a long pipeline which ran above the cows for the length of the cowshed. This pipeline was attached to a vacuum pump driven by an electric motor which created the suction necessary to draw out the milk from the udders just like a suckling calf. At the centre of the pulsator was a small glass dome through which you could see the milk flow. This allowed the farmer to see when the milk had stopped flowing so he could detach the cups.

Full buckets were taken to the cooling house, which was alongside the cowshed, and poured into a tank that sat on top of a concertina shaped stainless steel contraption called a cooler which looked a bit like an open but narrow piano accordion. This had cold water running inside it and the milk would be cooled as it ran down the outside of the concertina shape into the individual ten gallon churns. These would be put out in the late evening on the milk stand for collection early the following morning by a flatbed lorry that had chains around the sides to stop the churns falling off and empty churns were left in their place. All the cows would be let out at the same time and another group would come in for their turn. Once complete the next job was to clean the cowshed of all the muck produced and put it on the dung heap. We were usually allowed down once all the cows had gone but tended to keep out of the way when the messy cleaning was done. We did however 'get in the way' when the cooling house was being washed as Brynley would throw buckets of water over the cleaned concrete and we invariable got in the way and ended up going home soaking wet.

Mary and Glyndwr outside the cow shed

Brynley and Jack also fulfilled the role of the local milkman. Before the advent of the milk bottle, milk would be carried down to Rhoshill in a churn and Brynley or Jack would use a ladle to serve the milk into whatever container the residents supplied. Milk would be supplied to the residents of Rhoshill and to other dwellings north and south of the village. A tin box would be left outside the shop for payment and this could be left all day before collection. The correct amount was always included showing total honesty from the community. Once bottles were introduced a crateful would be left outside the shop and each week the total payment would be placed in the tin. Of course there was no choice then, we would all have full fat creamy milk – no skimmed or semi skimmed. We would collect our milk daily from Wenvoe as would Mair for Rhiwgoi, while Gordon Allison would usually collect the milk for Sychpant during the times when they didn't have milking cows.

Most of the cows were bred on the farm. A bull would be brought in regularly and there were always a number of pregnant cows. This ensured that they could continue to produce milk. Watching a calf being born was awesome. The calves were reared in their own shed and once big enough the males would be sold on for eventual meat production or, for the lucky few, calf production. Most of the females were kept as milking cows but sometimes there was a surplus which would be sold.

Much of the land was used for grazing and the rest was either just left fallow or was used for crop production, the main crops being hay, wheat and later silage. One field or part of a field, which we called **parc tato** (potato field), was always set aside for growing vegetables mostly potatoes but also peas, beans, carrots and cabbages. I don't remember much about hay making in the 1950s but I do have vivid memories of the wheat harvest. In the early 1950s the wheat was cut by a binder which had a cutter on the front and the wheat would be guided into the machine which would produce sheaves (a bundle of grain stalks tied together). These were gathered together into a stook (several sheaves leaning against each other) in order to fully dry. Once dry the sheaves were loaded onto trailers and taken to be stacked in the farmyard. Threshing of the corn was done later in the winter months. The contractor, who made the rounds of local farms, would arrive with the threshing machine, which was driven by a traction engine. The threshing machine was invented in England in the late eighteenth century to separate the wheat grains from the stalks. As with any new mechanical invention this cause a great deal of unemployment amongst farm workers and even led to riots. Again threshing (**dyrnu**) would be a big event with the various farms getting together to help and the farmers' wives keeping everyone going with hot tea and food. I remember threshing machine being big, noisy and scary and I kept well away but was nevertheless very excited. The sheaves would be thrown on top of the machine into a collection box; one or two labourers worked on top of the machine to cut the string off the sheaves and feed them into the machine. The grain would come out at one end and be poured into sacks while the straw came out at the other end and would be moved for storage in a barn for use as bedding during the winter months for any animals that were inside. The threshing machine was replaced during the 1950s by the combine harvester and baler so that the harvest became a lot less labour intensive once more. You now needed one person to drive the combine harvester and another to fill the sacks. He would stand on a platform behind the driver and fit the sacks over the shutes out of which came the grain which had been separated from the straw. The straw, meanwhile, came out of a large chute at the back in a straight row ready to be baled. However, labourers were still required to collect the sacks of wheat and the bales of straw from the fields, load them onto trailers and store them in farm buildings.

The Binder

The wheat is placed in stooks prior to collection

A Threshing Machine

At Wenvoe, the grain was taken to the **ysgubor**, which directly translated means barn, but it wasn't like you would imagine a traditional barn to be. It had a proper sloping slate roof and thick stone walls with a few small windows. It was typical of the sort of building that these days we would see as a barn conversion and in fact many years later it was converted to an extra home on the site. The rear entrance of the **ysgubor** was at one level and the front entrance was at a lower level. This allowed the sacks of grain to be taken in through the back door and stored upstairs without having to be carried up any steps. In the middle of the storage area there was a grinder. The grain could be easily fed into the grinder's hopper which appeared through a hole cut in the floor and the ground grain (meal) would appear downstairs at the other end of the machine and filled yet more sacks. Mixed with milk this formed the basis of the winter feed especially for the young calves and pigs.

Alongside the **ysgubor** was a huge building, what I would call a 'traditional' barn, used for storing bales of hay. Hay harvesting was probably the busiest time of the year and the whole community got involved, it was labour and machinery intensive and the local farmers would help each other. They did however for much of the 1950s have to hire a baling machine (baler) and Jim Rhyd (where he lived not his surname!) was the man to hire as he had two balers! Toward the end of the 1950s Allison Sychpant bought his own baler so he didn't have to join the queue for Jim Rhyd's services, so his main contribution to the harvest involved baling the hay at Sychpant and at Wenvoe.

Allison's first baler made round small bales, but this was soon replaced by a machine which produced the more familiar square bale. Allison designed and built a wooden hay sledge which had a hinged back half, this was towed behind the baler on which one man (often Jack Wenvoe) would stand and, using a special hook which Allison had fashioned from a cut down hay fork, he would stack the bales in fours as they were discharged by the baler and then he lifted the handle to tip them off. We children would love to ride on the hay sledge sitting on the bales and enjoying being tipped off, our legs were always covered in scratches from landing on the prickly hay stubble. Having the bales in groups of four cut down on a lot of leg work when it came to stooking them later on. Stooking involved leaning together four or more bales at a slight angle so that any rain would run off the bales. This was done to further dry and season the hay for several days before it was gathered in on flatbed trailers to be stored in the hay barns. The harvest usually started in late June and would often go on until the middle of August. My memory of what happened when, during the early 1950s, the late 1950s and early 1960s is a little blurred. However whichever date it was, hay making involved four processes, cutting or mowing; raking and turning; baling (or before balers were introduced gathering the loose hay together for collection) and finally collection and storage. More and better machinery was introduced as the 1950s and 1960s progressed.

The cutting involved a tractor with an attached cutting machine/mower with a blade about six feet long which resembled a large hedge trimmer. The tractor was driven up and down the field cutting rows of grass. As this was still very green it had to be left to dry for, depending on the weather, several days. During this time it was turned and fluffed up by a raking machine. Once the hay was considered dry enough, the tractor-towed baler produced bales that looked like giant bricks which were stoked for a few more days to dry. The bales were usually light enough to be lifted by an average farm worker and collected from the field by tractor and trailer, although as the layers on the trailer got higher it would need two people to lift the bales and for the top few layers pitchforks would have to be used. The bales would be lifted onto the trailer by farm hands and other seasonal labour. It was a long working day. If the weather was right the day would run from early morning until it was dark. Of course you couldn't start very early if there was dew on the ground but on a fine day things would soon dry up.

The hay barn was probably the biggest building on the farm. It was basically a structure of metal girders supporting a curved corrugated iron or zinc roof. Bales would be stacked in here during harvest and the hay would feed the cattle throughout the winter. The bales were packed to a height of well over fifteen feet using an elevator/lifter. About four feet of headroom was left at the top. For us, this provided a great place to play, especially as the bales were gradually removed for feeding, producing a step formation leaving it easier to climb to the very top. Up here was warm, dry and cosy and made a great place for a picnic. It was essential that the bales were stored in the right condition. If too green they would sweat and possibly rot or even overheat and cause a fire - one of the farmers' biggest fears.

Another time when farmers got together was the potato harvest which took place in the autumn. It was not such a big event as the other two harvests and would usually be over in a day depending on how much help neighbours would provide. The children would help, walking behind the harvesting machine picking up potatoes and placing them in sacks. Unlike the adults we didn't stick at this for very long as it was hard back breaking work. We did however join in with the adults when the tea and food arrived. Otherwise we would be playing in the potato field or surrounding fields or digging up and eating carrots. Sacks of potatoes would be stored in a dry place over winter in the hope that they would last until early the following summer. As already mentioned we had a couple of rows of potatoes in Wenvoe's field to add to those earlies that dad grew in Brynislwyn.

Towards the late 1950s Brynley and Jack decided to build a new shed to store silage. Again this was a large structure of metal girders supporting a curved zinc roof similar to the hay barn but with concrete block walls for half its height on either side and with a concrete floor and double gates at the front. As it was built into the sloping farmyard the back wall was also made of concrete blocks but once the silage pit was full you could walk onto its top directly from that part of the yard. Silage is basically green grass which is collected immediately after cutting and stored as a big heap under cover while it turns itself into nutritious cattle feed. How the cows could eat the brown, wet awful smelling stuff I don't know. When they needed to start using the silage they cut away slices with a large saw and carted it away in wheelbarrows. The first cut gradually removed a six foot wide slice from the centre of the silage heap, at the bottom of which was a layer of wet dark brown smelly slurry covering the concrete floor.

Never one to resist a challenge I decided one day that I could jump across this gap. It was roughly a six foot gap and a six foot drop into the slurry. There wasn't much of a run up but I managed to get my feet to land on the other side. Unfortunately, I landed with a sixty degree lean backwards and slowly fell into the slurry. It was a hard landing onto the concrete floor but I was more concerned that I was covered in muck. There was a major rollicking when I got home and a hose down before I was allowed into the house for a bath. In late autumn this wasn't a pleasant experience. Needless to say no other punishment was required and I didn't try that jump again.

We made full use of the fields surrounding the farm for exploring and foraging and would often help Brynley or Jack and the dog drive the cows for grazing after milking. We also loved going to collect them but this was pretty easy as once the gates were opened the cows knew their way to the milking shed. Most of the time after milking the cows could walk straight out of the farmyard towards one of the surrounding fields but sometimes they would be sent to Ty Newydd which involved a walk down the hill past our house. You could guarantee that the cows would empty their bowels on the road on the way down and on the return journey and walking on the road became a little tricky during these times.

One of Brynley's favourite phrases was 'Haven't you got a home to go to?' which was made in jest but reflected the amount of time we used to spend on the farm which no doubt was a big help for my mother when my sister was born. We were always reluctant to go home, even to go to the toilet. Once I waited until I was desperate and it was too late to run home so I disappeared behind the hedge which separated one of the fields from the farmyard. Half way through, with my trousers around my ankles, Brynley marched past followed by three or four children. I was mortified, although no-one took much notice. There was an outside toilet at the back of Wenvoe's house so I don't know why I didn't use it, too embarrassed to ask I suppose, I certainly wasn't too shy. We even spent time in their parlour watching the small black and white television. The Lone Ranger and Champion The Wonder Horse were big favourites. We were once banned from watching the television due to the unfortunate smells produced which no one would admit to. I know it wasn't me and my brother insisted it was the farmer's daughter Mary, but I'm not so sure. I remember we cried and begged my mother to go and ask if we could return but to no avail. She said we only had ourselves to blame but we were allowed back in after a couple of weeks. It was a few more years before we got our own television.

Life on the farm, as I've described it sounds idyllic and it's easy to forget that working farms can be dangerous places. A few incidents will serve to illustrate. When she was about eleven Jean Allison was wandering around the farm when she noticed a sow and her litter of piglets rooting about the farmyard. She saw that one of the piglets had become separated from its mother so she cornered it and picked it up in order to return it to its mum. As she picked it up it squealed and in an instant the sow charged and attacked her. She dropped the pig and ran but the mother continued to attack. Fortunately Jack had seen the whole event unfolding and as the sow charged he ran towards Jean and managed to beat off the sow. This was a terrifying experience but apart from some teeth punctures, grazes, torn clothes and obviously shock, she avoided serious harm thanks to Jack's timely intervention.

Another time (27 December 1962) we all went sledging on one of Wenvoe's steep sloping fields which were covered by a good layer of snow. This was the winter of the big blizzards and freezing conditions (1962/3) when we could trial our home made sledges. John's sledge was a particular beauty with polished metal runners fashioned from an old bed frame. The run from the top of the field to the bottom was probably about a hundred yards. Jean and Mary got on John's sledge and suddenly took off down the slope. Instead of turning as they approached the bottom they carried straight on and went over the hedge onto the road below. Despite it being covered with a layer of snow, it was a heavy fall and both were badly bruised and shaken but fortunately there were no broken bones. On the same field during one harvest Gordon Allison was baling hay and while normally he would go across the slope, for some reason he went downwards on this occasion. Now the baler is a pretty powerful

64

machine and when baling at full power puts a lot of strain on the tractor pulling it and in this instance the tractor and baler started running out of control down the slope. It could have developed into a nasty situation but fortunately Gordon was able to gradually turn before reaching the bottom and disaster was averted. Also potentially dangerous was the plague of rats that invaded Wenvoe in the early 1970s. There were hundreds and they were everywhere but eventually due to the efforts of the local rat catcher they managed to get rid of them. Meanwhile Mary and Glyndwr had great fun using them as target practice with their father's air rifle.

When Brynley and Peggy retired, the children did not wish to take over the farm and so it was sold. Some of the land was bought by Sychpant and the house and outbuildings sold separately. Today there are two dwellings on the plot, the original farmhouse and another one created by converting the **ysgubor**. Wenvoe farmhouse once featured on Escape to The Country and by this time the loft had been converted into an extra bedroom with a huge window at the gable end which afforded incredible views over the countryside toward Cardigan Bay.

****

The Allison family moved to Sychpant from Yorkshire in the spring of 1950. They had bought Sychpant at an auction in Cardigan a few months earlier. Gordon Allison had been farming in partnership with his brother in the Vale of York. Margaret Allison was from Leeds, and had trained as a secretary before becoming a nurse during the war years. They had two daughters, Jean and Cathy, when they moved and John was born in Cardigan hospital in June of 1950. At this time Cathy was one and Jean was two so quite a hand-full for their parents on top of a major move.

The house was relatively new having been built in the 1930s and while it had electricity it had no running water or inside bathroom. Water had to be carried from a pump located in a field across the road behind the old byre (cow shed). The remains of the old house stood across the yard from the new house and were being used as a barn. At one end there was a pen containing a rather scary Friesian bull. The rest of the building was used for hay and mangold storage. A load of mangold (a root vegetable) would be delivered for winter cattle feed and this had to be chopped by turning by hand the handle of a special mangold/turnip chopper. There were few farm buildings other than the byre across the road, next to which was the milk stand where milk churns would be collected, just like at all the local farms, in the morning and empty churns left in their place. The milk was taken to a processing dairy in Newcastle Emlyn and from there by train via Carmarthen to various markets. In 1950 Sychpant was mostly a dairy farm of about eighty acres made up of lots of small fields surrounded by earthen hedges. Allison was always a canny and careful farmer so one of the first things he did was to hire a man with a bulldozer to remove many of these hedges to make larger and more productive fields. These earth hedges were full of rabbit burrows and foxes were a common sight stealing chickens, and later when they had sheep, newborn lambs. Dad was one of two rabbit catchers that were called in to deal with the large number of rabbits on the farm. Although dad only used traps the other one a Mr Mathias of Blaenpant Uchaf used ferrets to catch the rabbits. He would block as many of the entrances to the burrows as he could and then send in the ferrets. A lot of the rabbits were sold to a butcher in Cardigan and rabbit stew, which is delicious, was regularly consumed by all the local families.

Gordon and Margaret cleared the old house and orchard soon after taking over the farm, they then had a large Dutch barn erected with concrete block sides added at a later date, soon to be followed by a parallel extension. Later sheep were brought into the barn during lambing and, for the children, especially in winter, the barn was a great place to play, build dens or rig up a trapeze bar. While the Dutch barn was erected by outside contractors, all the other buildings were put up by Gordon and in later years with help from John. An extra cowshed was built just along from the house, a porch was added to protect the door to the house and the yard was concreted. Another shed was built alongside the barn extension to be used for rearing pigs. Later a bigger shed was built near this one and was high enough to park the cattle truck. This faced the yard and required the purchase of a very small corner of a field belonging to a neighbouring farm. During the late 1950's and early 1960s, whenever he was able to, Dad spent some time working at both Sychpant and Wenvoe. He helped with the hay harvest at both farms and at Sychpant he did some fencing and building walls. Gordon Allison was very skilful and all the work he did on the farm had to be very precise. I can remember being very impressed with the quality of fencing he produced which seemed much superior to any other I had seen but which was very necessary to make sure the sheep didn't escape.

Like us, the Allison children never ever got bored, spending time outdoors whatever the weather, helping on the farm and also in play activities. In the way that we had our **cwm** they had a stream starting as a deep ditch in one of their fields and running along their boundary and draining into a **cwm** which ran for a few miles. There was a wealth of history along this **cwm**, including a ruined village with the remains of a mill and its water wheel. In the spring, snowdrops, primroses, daffodils and later bluebells appeared. The local lanes also had an abundance of, and a huge variety of, wild flowers plus the tiny sweet wild strawberries in summer. Then in autumn there would be blackberries to collect and hazel nuts which were usually cracked between two stones. There were various abandoned and ruined cottages to explore along all the lanes and often there were still productive gooseberry bushes in these overgrown and ruined gardens. Various tramps would come round once a year carrying their meagre possessions in a sack. At Sychpant they would knock on the door and ask for a cup of tea and a bite to eat and also request permission to sleep overnight in the barn.

Sometimes they would help out with the odd job or two. There was also **Sioni Wynwns** (Jonnie Onions), a Frenchman from Brittany who wore a beret; he called on his bike selling onions from the strings of plaited and dangling from the handlebars. These were also regular visitors at Uncle Islwyn's pub where they were usually guaranteed to make good business. Convoys of army vehicles were regularly seen in the area; they had a base in Castle Martin in South Pembrokeshire, and occasionally even camped on Sychpant land complete with their camouflage nets.

To start with, the farm had a small dairy herd of mixed breeds which was gradually increased over the early years. Like all dairy cattle they were milked twice daily and kept indoors during the winter. Gordon was severely ill and in hospital in Swansea for several months in the mid 1950's, and as it was too hard for Margaret, with three young children, to manage the milking long term she sold the cows and when Gordon recovered he restocked with sheep, and then later started farming pigs. Eventually Gordon took up dealing - buying & selling livestock - and would regularly attend the local cattle markets. There was Cardigan cattle market on a Monday, Carmarthen on a Wednesday and Newcastle Emlyn on a Friday. In the mid 1950s he bought a good sized trailer and built in a second deck. He would often buy pigs locally and then take them on to sell at cattle markets in Hereford and Stratford Upon Avon. The children would have a day off school, usually a Wednesday, and they would all go as a family on these whole day excursions setting off between three thirty and four am. Jean says that seeing the sun rise over the Malvern Hills was a lasting memory and seeing all the orchards and hop fields with their oast houses was a real novelty. They always stocked up on fruit, peas and beans to bring back home with. They bought a deep freezer and it was the children's task to shell these many sacks of peas and beans ready to be blanched and frozen. There was an annual autumn sale in Cardigan market of the foals rounded up from the herd of wild ponies from the Preseli hills and one year Gordon bought the three children a foal each.

As the dealing business grew, Gordon, Jean and Jack Wenvoe went to buy a decommissioned army truck from somewhere in England. Gordon drove the truck back and Jack drove the car. Jack fell asleep at the wheel and ended up in a ditch, but he wasn't injured and the car didn't suffer too much damage and Gordon managed to tow it out with the truck. Gordon transformed the army vehicle into a cattle truck but eventually this improvised truck was replaced by purpose built ones allowing regular travel to England. These were the journeys that Dad would sometimes go on when it was time to sell our pigs. I can always remember Gordon's cattle truck regularly passing our house and I always felt that when he was going down the hill that anything coming in the other direction wouldn't stand much of a chance!

By the end of the 1960s John went away to college to do Teacher's Training. After a year he decided that teaching was not for him and he returned to Sychpant to farm with his dad and Cathy while he contemplated his future. While their dad continued with his dealing John and Cathy went into partnership to breed pigs and later fattening cattle as well as growing hay and wheat. In 1977 John and Cathy both married local spouses. Cathy wed a local farmer called Beyron Thomas and settled in Blaen y Rangell, about a mile up the lane past Penlanbridell. A few months before this, Gordon and Margaret had moved into a new bungalow they had built across the road from the farm and Gordon continued with his dealing while playing a lesser role on the farm. John decided to revert to dairy and the farm has expanded greatly since then. Today the farm is run by John and his wife Mair and his son and daughter-in-law Marc and Lucy and has been developed into a highly efficient state of the art modern dairy farm with quite a reputation in the area. It's probably over five times as big as it was in the 1950s, having expanded to include much local acreage. John and Marc have erected numerous new buildings themselves and have even installed their own wind turbine to power the farm.

In 2019 Sychpant won the Royal Welsh Farm Buildings competition for their USA Style Cow Barn. After a visit by a farmer from USA who provided some advice on their future in dairy, one of John's sons Thomas went over to the USA to see the set up there and when he came back they decided to build a modified version of this barn (as the weather was less extreme in West Wales) which could house three hundred cattle. Surprisingly, contrary to what you might expect cows prefer to be indoors, so although at Sychpant they often leave the doors open, to give them a choice, the cows might venture out, have a little excited run around, but then prefer to come back inside.

Jean and Cathy started at Bridell School together despite their age difference. At this time the school only had about thirty pupils which had dropped to just twenty by the time the Allison children left; it was closed just a few years later. The Wenvoe children also attended Bridell school which was little different from many other small local schools which served the area. It was a two classroom, solid, tall building made from grey slate slabs (probably from one of the quarries around Cilgerran) and protected from the road at the front by a stone wall, with tarmac yards at the back. School dinners were delivered from the larger school at Cilgerran in large insulated metals containers. In the summer the children played rounders in the farmer's field across the road and were also taken on regular rambles to the cwm behind the school, the same one that started at Sychpant, the one that the Allison children explored regularly. Christmas concerts were held at the nearby church hall as was the Coronation party of summer 1953.

In the early 1960s Mrs Boarst, a friend and close neighbour of the Allisons, who was a district nurse, persuaded Margaret to cover for another nurse who was on maternity leave. Margaret agreed but had to refresh her driving skills having not driven since the war years and she started off her rounds in a little blue Comer van. She enjoyed this experience so much that she decided to return to her old nursing school in Boscombe, to do a four month refresher nursing course. She then joined the district nursing service in the Cardigan, St Dogmaels and Newport areas which she continued for the next fifteen years. Jean followed in her mother's footsteps and trained as a nurse and from late 1966, when she spent six months as a nanny in Somerset before starting her nurse training; she mainly lived away from Sychpant. In 1975 she emigrated to Australia before moving on to New Zealand where she still lives with her husband and has four children and four grandchildren.

By the mid to late1950s we got to know John and Cathy quite well. We didn't spend much time at Sychpant but they would often come over to Brynislwyn and Wenvoe and we spent quite a bit of time playing together. Because she was older we didn't see Jean as much. She was friendly with a girl called Jennifer Payne who lived at Gerallt, located just opposite Windy Hill Farm, up the road from Rhoshill. Jean also spent more time at Wenvoe, especially after Mary was born as she loved babies and Peggy would let her take Mary for quite long walks in the pram on her own.

The Allison family had lots of contact with Wenvoe, especially with Jack but also with Peggy and Brynley, who were always a great support and very good friends to the Allisons, which was really appreciated. The children were constantly in and out of their house, Peggy regularly providing them with afternoon tea - fresh Pen Bont (the local bakery in Cardigan) thinly sliced bread and butter with cheese or jam, Welsh cakes, and a wonderful Victoria sponge cake. Peggy would slice the loaf holding it to her chest and cutting towards herself. There was always the concern she would cut herself, but she never did. Like us the Allison children enjoyed watching their television (nobody else nearby had one), and used to call after school to watch Blue Peter and other children's programmes, as well as having tea of course. Although they weren't particularly religious the Allison children often went to chapel at Ty Rhos, which was on the road to Cilgerran, with Brynley and Peggy and also to the annual singing festival called **Gymanfa Ganu** held at Ty Rhos and other local chapels.

We went to different schools. They went north to Bridell and we went south to Blaenffos. Initially, Jean and Cathy would be taken to and collected from school by their parents, but in the summer and when the weather was nice, they would walk home along the country lanes. By the time John started school they were picked up at Rhoshill by Mrs Rumble from Boncath who ran a taxi service. She would fit in as many as nine children from Rhoshill and the surrounding areas before dropping them off at school and collecting them at the end of the day. No seat belts then and apparently no accidents either. Of course there were far fewer cars on the road.

Quite often on their walk back from Rhoshill they would call in and join us for tea. There might well have been a bit of competition for the Allison kids between mam and Peggy, although we were at a disadvantage as we didn't have a television! We would always have a drink and cake and sometimes sandwiches when we got home, as we would be starving. We would then have a light supper a little time before going to bed. During the holidays and at weekends John and Cathy might be with us for a whole day and would thus stay for dinner. Apparently John thought that my mother's **cawl** was the best he had ever tasted. **Cawl** was a one pot meal made by slowly cooking a brisket of beef in water and seasoning to which, during the process, would be added a range of vegetables and potatoes. The combination of beef, fat, salt, pepper and vegetables would blend into a fabulous taste and it was also one of our favourites. It was served in two courses, first of all the beef stock was served as a clear broth in soup bowls, then the brisket was carved and served with the potatoes and vegetables and a little surplus liquid served as gravy. Apparently John nagged his mother to make some **cawl** which she eventually agreed to. When he thanked her for doing so she asked him if it was alright. It seems he told her that it was very nice but the problem was that she 'wasn't Welsh'!

John would often come with us when we went to the beach and at the end of the picnic, if there was any food left, he would politely ask 'would you like me to finish that for you'. John also had this trick with chickens. He would catch one, tuck her head under her wing and spin her around. He would then place her on the ground and the chicken would be so giddy that she would stumble like a drunk all over the place as she tried to run away. Early on there were chickens at Sychpant but they also suffered from Mr Fox as well as from their dog and in the end, like us, they had to give up. The very last chicken drowned when John, as a very young child, decided to see if chickens could swim and placed her in the cattle trough only to promptly wonder off and forget about her. He discovered that chickens cannot swim! Between animals and humans chickens really did have a tough time trying to survive in the countryside. At one stage we started a birds' egg collection. We were always careful to take no more than one egg and none if there were only one or two in the nest. Climbing trees was never a problem and once John climbed up to the top of the hay barn in Sychpant for an owl's egg and also scaled the cliffs at Lydstep for a seagull's egg.

From what has already been written it's clear that the four families of Brynislwyn, Wenvoe, Sychpant and Rhiwgoi were all very close. We would see each other more or less every day; we could all depend on each other if there was a crisis or if one family in particular needed extra help. As they lived so close to each other mam, dad, Brynley and Peggy were totally reliable and dependable if any one needed extra help. Gordon and Jack spent a lot of time together, dad and Jimmy did a lot of odd jobs and often when there were minor medical issues no doctor was required as Margaret Allison was a district nurse, always ready to provide the support needed. And of course the children spent a lot of time together. It was all fairly typical of how communities operated then.

There were a few other farms in the area which we got to know quite well. Two wheeler bikes allowed us to go a bit further and sometimes we would turn left before reaching Sychpant up another single track country lane. At the top of this lane and further along the road were a number of farms, one of which (Penlanbridell) we would occasionally visit. Five brothers lived on that farm with their parents Bill and Megan. The boys were Wyn, Glanedd, Derfel, Geraint and Dylan. Derfel and Geraint were the same age as my brother and I and we all went to the same school. Wyn, the oldest was quite a bit older than us and he soon opened a business as a mechanic repairing agricultural machinery, particularly tractors; this was located just down the road from the family farm. A little further along this road was the farm called Blaen y Rangell where Cathy and Beyron settled. Penlanbridell was on the southern border of Sychpant while on its northern border there was a large farm called Close owned by Arthur James and his wife Verona. They had geese wandering around their farm yard threatening any strangers who entered the yard, honking chasing and pecking them. I was later to spend one of my summers working at this farm. Arthur's brother Dewi lived on their bordering property called Oernant and he had three children. Dilwyn, the oldest became a butcher in Cardigan and renovated Bridell School when it closed down and changed it into a home for himself and his family. Both his sisters Eirian, who was good friends with Mary Wenvoe, and Buddig had excellent singing voices and went on to become professional singers, perhaps following in their father's footsteps as he had done quite a lot of part time acting and radio work.

Two other farms already mentioned were Windy Hill Farm owned by Carlo Frishgoni and Trip most of whose land bordered onto Wenvoe's and was also immediately north of Rhiwgoi, where Dan and Olwen lived. Finally another farm we knew fairly well was Cwmbettws where Tom and Doris Davies lived with their three children, Ann, Delyth and John. This farm is situated on the road to Eglwyswrw about a mile beyond Sychpant. Ann, who was also good friends with Mary, went to the same secondary school as us and married one of my school friends, Cerwyn and they still live on a farm south of Crymmych. John Davies still lives at Cwmbettws; at one time he was Chairman of Pembrokeshire County Council. He is still a county councillor and among other things he is Chairman of the Royal Welsh Show which is held every year at Builth Wells.

Christmas and Other Key Events

Like all children we looked forward to Christmas. One of the first things to do was put up the Christmas tree and we would make our own. We had a large evergreen bush growing on the bank above the kitchen window and the branches looked just like those of any normal Christmas tree, so dad would choose a section to cut and if necessary would cut other branches to tie to the main one until we had the classic shape of the tree. Making decorations for the tree and the house was next. We would buy a few over the years but part of the fun was making our own, a favourite and easy one being paper chains made from coloured paper and sellotape or glue. My parents always bought a big boxful of Cox's apples at Christmas, from a van that came around, and you could be sure of having an apple in your stocking along with a small orange, a small toy and a few nuts. Brazil nuts were a real treat but a nightmare to shell particularly if using a hammer. I can remember one year having a gun belt, gun and holster as a present and another time a Meccano set which was probably my favourite present. We also had Tonka toys, usually tractors and trailers which we would use in the garden to play farms. Once my brother and I each had a pair of boxing gloves, probably a mistake as I often ended up with a sore and sometime bloody nose. On Christmas Eve we managed to persuade mam and dad to let us have a go with the gloves and, to our surprise, they said yes. We did a bit of sparring and then I rushed at my brother, he ducked; I went over his shoulder and banged my forehead on the edge of the piano. The late hours of Christmas Eve were spent in the local hospital waiting for stitches to be inserted in the cut that had opened up just above my eye. That limited our boxing for a while but we were soon back at it. I was obviously a glutton for punishment as I usually ended up either in tears or in a temper from being hit so often and managing to land very few in return.

From the late 1950s when my father became a fire officer he would often work the day shift on Christmas Day as it paid double time. We

76

didn't really mind and we still had Christmas dinner but on Boxing Day. My mother cooked a superb roast dinner and Christmas dinner was no exception. We tended to have chicken rather than turkey, either one of our own or one from Wenvoe which meant that it didn't cost us anything. Christmas dinner came with all the trimmings with home-made Christmas pudding and white sauce for desert. In the run up to Christmas mam would cook several Christmas puddings; these would simmer away for hours in a great big water heater borrowed from Wenvoe. The main use for the heater was to boil enough water to make big jugs of tea for the workers during harvest time so borrowing it for a day in the run up to Christmas was no problem. The puddings were in white pudding basins covered with muslin cloths tied at the top as this made it easy to lift them out of the water. Up until quite recently we continued to have one of mam's Christmas puddings. Mam also made a superb trifle but this was usually reserved for special occasions, Christmas being one of those. Making the Christmas cake was also an event and we all got a go at turning the rich mixture and having a taste before its long slow bake in the oven. Having a fruit cake covered in marzipan and icing was a real treat. She must have been saving for months to provide such memorable Christmas feasts. Of course all these goodies would last several days so I suppose they were good value.

****

A major event, which stands out in my memory was Guy Fawkes Night. The four families, which included up to eleven children, were involved and as we got older we took a more active part in the preparations and on the night. The first stage was building a huge bonfire on our grounds between the well and the foot of the quarry. Suitable materials were collected over several weeks and as two of the families had farms there was no shortage of old wooden crates and pallets, paper, cardboard and old bags, as well as firewood which we collected from the surrounding area. Much of this was stored next door under cover until a few days before the fifth when we transferred it to the bonfire. Paper and cardboard was transferred as late as possible because you couldn't guarantee the weather.

The children made a Guy Fawkes from old clothes stuffed with paper and straw and placed it on top of the bonfire. Paper was stuffed into any gaps which existed between the timbers of the structure. All the families pooled their fireworks and these were kept out of the way in the workshop nearby. Often friends of the various families would turn up and bring extra fireworks. Catherine Wheels were attached to the shed walls or door frames and there were plenty of sparklers for the children to wave about. Once it was dark, all pets were safely indoors and an adult lit the bonfire and various adults would set off the fireworks. One firework we all loved, especially if thrown into a crowd was the Jumping Jack which, when set off would bang and jump around on the floor making people scream and jump, but it seemed quite safe (we thought so anyway). Mums would bring out trays of food and hot and cold drinks which we would have during a break in setting off the fireworks. The celebrations would last about two hours and it took the bonfire several hours to burn down and during this time we would sometimes place potatoes wrapped in foil into the ashes. One year a Catherine Wheel spun out of control and fell off its nail, on the workshop's wall, into the box containing the entire stock of fireworks which some idiot had left nearby. The lot went off in one spectacular show lasting less than a minute which put a bit of a dampener on the rest of the evening. Once the excitement had died down it was lovely sat within a safe distance of the warm flames on usually, a very cold night, before being packed off to bed. Before going home a few of the adults would stay to make sure that the fire went out safely and probably have a couple of drinks to while away the time.

Halloween is celebrated on 31 October but usually we didn't bother apart from once during our early years in secondary school. Lyndon and I had bought some large swedes; we hollowed them out and cut out eyes, a nose and mouth for each one. We got some candles and decide to walk across the fields to the main road running south to Crymmych just above Windy Hill Farm, we placed the swedes, each with a lighted candle inside, at the side of the road and Lyndon and John lay on the road alongside them, Jean, Cathy and myself were on the hedge above the road and I decided I would hang from a tree whenever a car approached in the distance. The first car to come along stopped and the man got out and gave us a major rollicking. He said that he thought there had been an accident and what we were doing was very dangerous. He was of course right and we went home in silence with our tails between our legs. Needless to say we didn't bother much with Halloween after that.

****

Most of the local villages held sports events during the summer usually as part of wider festivals. There would usually be a range of stalls and a very popular tug of war competition. Teams would come from several villages and pull against each other for a cash prize. One or two of the teams had quite a reputation and they would go around the villages taking on all comers. A team from Llanboidy in Carmarthenshire were particularly strong and for some years were rarely beaten. Sports were mainly for children and included running and cycle races as well as novelty races like three legged, egg and spoon and the sack race. I was pretty good at the sprints and cycle races, although didn't often win first prize. However in my age group I was pretty well unbeatable at the sack race. Although we loved the competition what we liked best were the money prizes which were handed out for first, second and third. It was a useful supplement to our pocket money.

Some towns and villages also put on carnivals where adults and children dressed up as well known characters and marched through the village before meeting in a field for the judging. There were also floats, usually dressed up trailers pulled by tractors or lorries and sometimes pick -up trucks. The carnival was often one of the events held during a week of celebration. One local village, Cilgerran was nationally renowned for its festival week in August which culminated (and still does) in its famous coracle races. These started in 1950 and are held along the Teifi River as it runs downstream in the shadow of Cilgerran Castle. People would come from all over the country to watch and compete. The coracle, originally named **cwrwgl** is a small almost round boat, very light being made of a thin flexible wooden frame (originally willow) covered, originally, by animal skin but later by canvas or calico. They are designed for one person who uses a paddle in a left to right motion while leaning over the front of the boat. Their use dates back over 2000 years to pre-Roman times, in the 1950s and 1960s they were extensively used for fishing. On the River Teifi, River Taf and River Towy they are still used for fishing. It is necessary to get a licence and the licensed coracle fishers work in pairs with a net between each coracle and hope to catch fish as they drift down the river using one handed paddling to control the craft. The day before the coracle races was carnival day. I have included earlier a photograph of our family standing on the street in Cilgerran watching the procession go by. We were all dressed in nice clothes, Lyndon and I in t-shirt and blazer and sporting one of dad's haircuts. Dad was holding Brenda who was probably about eight months old which would make it August 1957.

When we were older we would dress up as individual characters and join the parade and hope to win a prize. In the early 1960s we became heavily involved in producing floats for Cilgerran and other carnivals. Harvest would usually be over so we could have a trailer from Wenvoe for a week or so while we built our float. The trailer was parked near the workshop on our grounds and this workshop provided all the tools we needed. I think we started with Cowboys and Indians. John, Cathy, Lyndon, Mary, Tony, myself, Brenda and Glyndwr were dressed as cowboys and Indians and we decorated the trailer with a tepee and a totem pole. Costumes were reasonably straight forward, we had a range of cowboy hats and feathers were used for the Indian headgear. Some of us already had guns and bows and arrows, and bought costumes and any shortfall was made up from old sacking from Wenvoe and Sychpant. Our best creation was however Pirates. We painted sheets of zinc black and nailed them to the sides of the trailer and shaped them in such a way that they resembled the sides of a boat. As the trailer had an extension at the front which rose above the hitch this was perfect for a poop deck which we made out of planks of wood and on which the captain stood. We firmly attached a mast to this deck by drilling through the deck and tying the mast to the hitch below so the captain could hold on if need be when the trailer was moving. Another mast was attached to the main deck and as we couldn't drill a hole in the trailer's floor we put this in a barrel, attached to a block of wood and supported by rigging. One of the younger children was put in the barrel which was firmly attached to the deck. We also built a small cabin at the front of the trailer. Costumes for the pirates were a bit trickier than for cowboys and Indians but we managed with a bit of help from the grownups. We had hats, eye patches, swords and knives made out of wood, handkerchiefs with knots in made good pirate headgear but I don't remember there being a stuffed parrot. On the day of the carnival Brynley would attach the tractor to the trailer and he would drive us down the few miles to Cilgerran. We entered a float in Eglwyswrw and Cardigan carnivals but less often and we usually won first prize in most of the carnivals we entered.

The last one we did was a much simpler affair as we no longer had Lyndon, John and Cathy. This was Robin Hood and his Merry Men and involved attaching a lot of leaved branches to the sides, front and back of the trailer. Tony was Robin Hood, Brenda was Maid Marian, I was Little John, Mary was Friar Tuck, and Glyndwr, David and Peter were merry men. Costumes were fairly straight forward, sacking and long sleeved T shirts were died green. For weapons, Little John and Friar Tuck had wooden staves, Robin and his merry men had bows and arrows and Robin and one of the merry men (Glyndwr) had wooden swords. We only entered Cilgerran Carnival that year but by now our fame had spread and we were invited to take part in the Whitland Carnival. They sent a pickup truck for us to decorate on the morning of the carnival, it was a bit of a rush but we still had our costumes and so we managed it. We weren't entered for any competition, they just wanted us as part of the parade through the village and they presented us all with silver cups before bringing us back to Brynislwyn.

Robin Hood and His Merry Men

Cilgerran was our nearest village of any size, the castle dates from about 1100. At one time its main industries were farming, fishing and slate quarrying. There were several quarries located mostly near the river and the slate was taken to Cardigan by boat and by the railway. In the 1950s it had a railway station, post office, garage and petrol station, general stores, a few small shops including one selling pet food, several public houses and a combined doctor and dentist. I do remember sitting in the doctor's waiting room a couple of times but don't remember what for. I can remember when Lyndon and I had Chicken Pox and Mary came over to share our bed over a few days so she could catch it. I can also vividly remember a visit to the dentist to have a couple of teeth removed – possibly wisdom teeth. This involved the administration of gas and a floating sensation from which I emerged with a lot of blood in my mouth and very groggy. I remember it took quite a while in bed at home to come round properly and I was sick more than once. We didn't visit the dentist very often and nor do I remember cleaning my teeth regularly which probably explains why I have a mouthful of fillings now.

The general store in Cilgerran, run by Mr Cole, was situated near the castle and this is where we got most of our groceries from. A list would be sent and a day or two later the items would be delivered but eventually when we got a car we could go to the shop to collect the groceries. We also had a grocery van come around once a week with a limited stock. We would get a weekly treat of some sweets either from Mr Cole's shop or from the van. We also bought Corona from the van and he would take back Corona bottles for which he would pay three pence. We would do our best to collect as many of these as we could to provide a bit of extra money. A butcher would also call around selling meat out of his car boot and a Walls ice cream van would venture up the road quite regularly. There was an occasional visit from a mobile hardware shop selling overalls, brushes, wellington boots etc. Now and again gypsies would call, the women selling such things as wooden clothes pegs and the men, who we referred to as Tinkers, would offer to fix pots and pans.

****

Towns and villages also had **eisteddfodau** (music and poetry festivals). These varied from small scale local events to national ones like the Welsh National **Eisteddfod** (open to all ages) and the **Urdd** National **Eisteddfod** (open to the youth of Wales). The Cardigan **Eisteddfod** was quite a big event with people coming from all over Wales where as the Boncath **Eisteddfod** was a small local event. I can remember taking part in the Boncath **Eisteddfod**; I played the piano and did a recitation of a comic poem. I'm pretty sure that as well as the glory of winning, there were money prizes involved which was always a good incentive. I remember winning the recitation and the judge commented that I looked the part being a bit of a scruffy looking rogue with my head at an angle and a naughty smile on my face during the performance of a light hearted poem. At the Cardigan **Eisteddfod** we had to take part in preliminary rounds first and the top four from these rounds would perform on the stage in the big pavilion. One year, in the piano playing competition for my age group, I managed to make it to the stage, which was pretty nerve wracking. I ended up fourth but was told that the experience was good for me!

Piano lessons figured in our lives in the 1950s and early 1960s. We would be taken to the teacher's house in Cardigan once a week. She was a little mouse of a thing but very strict and scary. We had to leave a pair of slippers inside her back door and when we arrived had to change out of our shoes and wash our hands before going into her front room where we had our lesson. One of us would sit on a towel on the couch while the other one had his lesson. We did our best to control any wind we might be fermenting. These lessons petered out in the 1960s when we went to secondary school and got involved in other interests, particularly sport. However we did manage to achieve level five which was pretty good for our age. We were however, quite reluctant to practice at home but mam kept us at it. It was agreed that we would do a maximum of half an hour of practice a day and it didn't matter at what stage we were in a piece of music, once the half hour was up we would get up and go. As practice was a constant battle I think mam was happy with that and didn't nag us too much to finish what we were playing.

Another event which we used to celebrate was **Calennig**. This is the Welsh word meaning New Year celebration/gift but literally it translates as 'the first day of the month'. No surprise then that **calenning** happened on the first of January each year and it was our way of celebrating New Year's Day, known in Welsh as **Dydd Calan**. On New Year's Eve we were allowed to stay up late to see in the New Year. Traditionally we would go out of the back door and be welcomed in through the front door with a gift, usually a piece of coal. This was a tradition that affected your luck for the rest of the year. Ideally the first one in after midnight should be a tall dark-haired man as he would bring good luck. Well we didn't have a tall one so had to make do with a short dark-haired man. Despite the late night we would get up early on New Year's Day so we could collect **calennig**. We got on our bikes and visited as many neighbours as we could before twelve noon. We would knock on the door, sing a short verse in Welsh which reminded them that it was the first day of the year, wishing them a happy new year and asking for a penny or a piece of bread and some cheese. The words are quite familiar and the verse one of only a handful of poems I can still remember.

Dydd Calan gynta'r flwyddyn, flwyddyn, flwyddyn

Dydd Calan gynta'r flwyddyn

Rwy'n dyfod ar eich traws

I ofyn am y geiniog, geiniog, geiniog

I ofyn am y geiniog a chlwt o fara caws

Blwyddyn Newydd Dda.

Most were very generous and would actually expect us to turn up, and were ready with gifts of fruit, sweets, chocolate or coins but not bread and cheese. As we had bikes, one year we went as far as the Pantyderi, the big mansion where dad used to do his rabbit trapping, as we thought they were rich and would be very generous. It was a wasted journey; despite singing at three different doors we got no reply. Perhaps they were still recovering from New Years Eve celebrations. Jean notes in her diary that on New Year's Day 1963 John, Cathy, Lyndon and I earned ten shillings and one penny each. This was another one of all the money making opportunities we had during the year.

****

Cardigan and Crymmych hosted fairs, which were very similar. Cardigan Fair was held in November and was bigger while Crymmych Fair was held on August Bank Holiday. Right from an early age through to our late teens we would rarely miss these fairs. They were characterised by their cacophony of sounds and noise, bustle, smells, shouting, music and lights. At the heart of the fair was 'Parc y Fair' which was the field where the main part of the fair was held. At Crymmych it was a farmer's field accessible off the main square. The Crymmych Arms and Village Hall occupied two of the corners of the square and the hall was full of stalls as was the road up to the main field and the roads leading off the square. You could buy virtually anything and the prices were much less than we were used to paying. In fact many of the stalls would auction their products and it was very entertaining just listening to the banter of the stall holders. They would sell meat, fish, fruit, crockery and kitchen equipment. My parents always bought a big box of plums and when we were a little older we would always buy our own bag of plums and eat most of them during the evening and not travel very far from the toilet the day after. The smell of hot dogs and onions was fantastic and we would always have at least one of these, or a burger, or sometimes both. You could also buy candy floss, toffee apples and a whole range of sweets. This was the only time of the year when we would see coconuts. If we failed to win one at one of the stalls we would be sure of buying one before going home. At the main field there were up to five rides, the waltzer, merry go round or carousel, swing boats, dodgems and the ghost train. The cars on the waltzer went up and down and spun round and there would always be two or three fairground lads who would go from one car to the other and give them and extra spin, especially if they had girls in them which would guarantee plenty of screaming. The swing boats needed two people to operate them, they had two seats opposite each other, metal rods were attached at one end to each corner of the boat and at the other end to the top of the structure, you had to pull at ropes attached to a piece of wood on a pulley also at the top of the structure and the harder you pulled the higher the boat would go. And that was our aim to get the boat to go beyond the horizontal which was just about possible. When your time was up the attendant would put the brake on which was a long piece of wood which they would lift up and jam against the bottom of the boat.

The dodgems or bumper cars were a particular favourite, they were small two seater electric cars which ran on power drawn from the floor and ceiling and although the idea was to dodge other cars most people would make every effort to ram them. Usually just as you had someone in your sights and were about to ram them someone would hit your back end and send you in a completely different direction. Sometimes there would be traffic jams when every car got snarled up and the attendants had to jump on the cars to turn the wheels in the direction required to ease the jam. These attendants would run back and fore on the metal floor jumping on the back of cars as necessary and would grab the steering wheel to avoid a collision or to get the driver out of trouble. Meanwhile the music was blaring through the loud speakers which together with the smell of the electric all added to the atmosphere. At the end of your allotted time the controller would turn the power off and you had to leave the ride unless you paid for another one.

The merry go rounds tended to be for younger children and consisted of animals or cartoon characters which we would sit on and go round and usually up and down gently. For younger children the ghost train was quite scary but for teenagers it was pretty tame. The two seater carriage would bang its way through the doors at the start of the ride and run along the track in the dark unless a light would flash and display a skeleton of ghostly figures. String or material dangled from the ceiling like cobwebs to touch your face and together with ghostly sounds had the desired effect on the little ones. The teenagers would just find it amusing, but quite a good one to take a girlfriend on. In fact taking a girlfriend on a date to the fair seemed quite popular with teenagers. These rides were surrounded by stalls where you could win prizes by shooting, throwing darts, throwing balls into a bucket, rolling coins and other ingenious ways of taking money off you. If you were lucky you might hit a coconut but even then there was no guarantee you would knock it over. A better bet was to try and knock a stack of tins off the shelf; at least this gave you a decent chance of winning the prized coconut but of course the macho one was to knock the coconut off its shy.

A big crowd was always attracted to watch men and boys pitting their skill and strength on the High Striker. This attraction had a metal pad which sat on a base, a puck was attached to the pad by a lever and when the pad was hit by a long handled mallet it would send the puck up a groove in a tower with the aim of hitting the bell at the top. The tower could be up to twenty foot high and the idea was the harder you hit the pad the more likely you were to hit the bell. Like many things the striker's skill in hitting the pad was just as important as the power put into the blow and several powerful looking chaps had their egos dented by the skill of smaller individuals. Apparently it is possible to adjust the tension on the lever so that the attendant may well have had an influence on the outcome. There was no prize but what red blooded male would not be chuffed with the ding of the bell as it was hit by the puck. Bingo was also very popular with the players, mostly female this time, seated around a circular stall with the caller in the middle surrounded by all the prizes.

As mentioned earlier Cardigan Fair was held in November and was a bit bigger than Crymmych. Stalls started on Finch Square which meant it could not be used for busses for at least three days by the time it was set up and cleared away. From here the road leading north from Finch Square to a large car park was lined with stalls as was the road which ran at right angles off this road along the north side of the car park. The car park itself was the main fairground where all the rides were located, with the dodgems in the centre. Today this car park houses the swimming pool as well as still having plenty of parking spaces. As with Crymmych the atmosphere was great with the same noise, bustle and smells plus lots more lights which were needed due to the time of year. Cardigan Fair also had a boxing ring where locals could take on the travelling pugilists.

The Summer Holidays

Before going to school life seemed to be one long holiday. However, once in school, the summer holidays were probably the highlight of the year (or possibly after Christmas and birthdays). Most years my Uncle Trevor (Mam's brother) and Auntie Eluned from North Wales would come and stay for a fortnight. My earliest memory of them is arriving on a scooter at the end of a 120 mile, eight hour journey. Two adults and luggage on a scooter for such an epic journey was quite an achievement. These days by car you could do the journey in about three hours. They did have a daughter, Alwena, who was older than us but until they got a car, they left her with her maternal grandparents who lived next door to them in a little village called Upper Llandwrog. I remember recently my auntie telling me that they had to plan the journey very carefully as they only had a small petrol tank and there weren't that many garages along the way. The scooter was fine on level ground and especially so downhill but on some hills she would have to get off and walk to make sure that the scooter got to the top and wouldn't run out of petrol. She remembers one long steep hill in particular, near Machynlleth when the petrol was running low. She had to get off and walk and her husband Trev. waited for her at the top of the hill. She was walking up dressed in a blue leather coat and blue helmet and the few cars which passed her honked their horns and whistled, thinking that they had had a quarrel and she had been left to walk!

These two weeks were always full of fun and laughter. We would regularly go to the beach and we would all manage to fit into two cars, ours and my grandfather's. For one such journey to Poppit we all wanted to go in **dadcu's** car. That was three adults and three children so mam and dad went on their own in their car. On the way to Poppit sands we had to negotiate a steep hill at St Dogmaels. For some reason **dadcu** had stopped and could not get going again and the car kept rolling backwards, which was no use. Dad had stopped at the top of the hill and mam came back to help. Although she didn't really drive, she managed to get the car going and got out at the top of the hill. **Dadcu** took over but by this time dad had gone and mam was left to walk the rest of the way. When we realised we stopped and managed to squeeze her into the car. There didn't seem to be any rules about overcrowding then, or else they were just ignored. During their stay with us, Trev. Being a talented carpenter often produced a small piece of furniture like the cupboard in the **llaethdy** or a small table or garden bench. He also enjoyed going off with his shotgun and always brought back a few rabbits or pigeons which were very tasty but had to be eaten carefully because they inevitably included some buckshot! He enjoyed taking pot shots at the pigeons that tended to sit in the large trees which were opposite our house at the bottom of Wenvoe's garden.

Picnics were also a regular thing and we would have a few during this fortnight. Mam would pack hot water in flasks; take a teapot and tea leaves, milk and sugar. Then there would be a large loaf and bread knife plus ingredients for sandwiches and also a range of cakes, and always a home-made tart. She much preferred this to preparing everything at home. An enjoyable evening pastime was playing cards and the favourite game was Horses. Our next door neighbours Brynley and Peggy usually came round and joined in. This was serious gambling! Stakes were high, pennies, halfpennies and three pence pieces, even occasionally a six pence piece. Two aces were placed in the centre of the table and you had to bet on either one of the aces and also place a bet in the kitty in between. The cards were dealt, and were put down on the table by the players in order starting with the two and finishing with aces or kings. The objective was to have the kings of the same suite as the aces on the table, in which case you won the money that had been placed on the cards and/or get rid of all your cards in which case you won the kitty. If the kitty was won before the kings, the stakes were left on the cards for the next game. As the value built up things could get quite heated. We thought that it was great that we were allowed to play and be exposed to the vices of gambling!

We would go to local beaches at other times outside this fortnight. We were lucky to have so many within five to ten miles of our home on the North Pembrokeshire and South Cardiganshire Coast. Poppit, Cwm Yr Eglwys, Mwnt and Llangrannog were probably our favourites. I remember that the latter had fabulous breakers which we loved jumping into and over, what a shame that we knew nothing about surfing then, I suspect we would somehow have made our own wooden surfing board. We would always have a picnic and make a day of it and of course it was essential to bring a bucket of sand and shells home. The road into Llangrannog was quite steep and mostly single track. The village of Llangrannog was a ribbon development which stretched out along the road with a few houses near the beach. Driving out of Llangrannog uphill in a little Austin Seven was tricky. Once we had to stop to give way to a car coming down the hill and dad had difficulty doing a hill start. The car kept slipping back, fortunately towards the hedge rather than down the hill. However we weren't getting anywhere fast so mam decided to put a saucepan behind the wheel which had kindly been provided by the family in the car behind us. It did the trick and dad managed to get the car going. The crushed saucepan was duly returned to its owners!

The beach we visited most often was Poppit Sands, on the South Cardigan Bay Coast, probably because it was the closest. To get there we had to drive down to Cardigan, turn left at the Eagle Inn towards St Dogmaels and uphill through the village where dadcu had problems getting up with a car full of North Walians, then right onto Poppit Road which ran parallel with the River Teifi for about two miles. We were always full of anticipation along this stretch as we could see glimpses of the river and then sand dunes as we approached the beach car park. Poppit was a huge expanse of sand backed by sand dunes and also a large area of rocky pools which were only exposed when the tide was out and boy could the tide go out. The beach had a huge tidal range and it was wide and flat so even when you got into the sea you had to walk quite a bit further to get to a decent depth. Here again the breakers could be pretty good but not a patch on Llangrannog. When the tide was coming in it used to move pretty fast and this was the best time to go into the sea because the breakers were decent and you could dive through them without being in any danger. However to the right of the beach was the Teifi estuary and you had to keep well away because the sand was soft and the current was strong.

Mam Lyndon, Brenda, Alan and Cousin Christine at Poppit

Mwnt beach was a bit further along the Cardigan Bay coast between Poppit and Llangrannog. Mwnt is a small secluded, sheltered sandy beach accessible by a steep path which is a combination of steps and pathway, with a small café part way down. It wasn't easy and took a fair amount of effort particularly on the way back up but it was worth it. The tidal range here is much smaller and at high tide the amount of room left on the beach is quite limited. When the tide is out, even though the range is small, it makes a significant difference. A clear landmark when you approach the beach is the small white Holy Cross Church which is thought to be dated from the fourteenth century. Mwnt gets its name from Foel y Mwnt, the large conical shaped hill that overlooks the beach on its North side.

Lyndon and Alan at Mwnt beach and ready to go.

We were also very keen on Cwm-yr-Eglwys. To get there we had to drive westwards from Brynislwyn up the lane towards and past Eglwyswrw on the A487 Cardigan to Fishguard road which runs along the North Pembrokeshire coast. The first decent beach off this road is Newport Sands which we would visit occasionally. It is a large flat sandy beach backed by sand dunes and is where the River Nevern enters the sea; it's a bit like Poppit and just as nice but on a slightly smaller scale. Another mile or so further on and we would turn right down another single track road which ended at Cwm-yr-Eglwys village and beach (translated as valley of the church). The beach, like Mwnt, was small and sheltered from westerly winds by Dinas Island peninsula but unlike Mwnt, the road to the beach was flat and the access from the small car park undemanding. It was nice and sandy and again a small stream flowed into the sea over one side of the beach, small enough to paddle in unlike the Teifi and Nevern rivers. At the back of the beach is a high protective stone wall which was probably built following an enormous storm in 1859 which washed away most of the village's twelfth century chapel so that all that is now left is the end wall with its bell tower. Cwm yr Eglwys also attracts boating and water sports enthusiasts as it has a slipway and boat club. Across the neck of the peninsula is another beach called Pwll Gwaelod (bottom pool) another small but nice sandy beach although, being the western side of the headland, is not as sheltered.

On a few occasions we also visited Tenby and Saundersfoot. This was a real treat because these towns were so much bigger and further than the others and even at that time a bit more commercialised, especially Tenby. You could say that Tenby has four beaches North Beach, South Beach, Castle Beach and Harbour Beach although you could also argue that there are only two beaches. North Beach is the one we tended to use most, it is a long stretch of golden sand overlooked by the town and promenade and you have to walk down a fairly steep slope to get to hit. This beach runs into Harbour Beach which is small and sheltered with a breakwater and lots of small boats anchored but we didn't think it was as good for swimming or playing in the sand as North Beach. Castle Beach backs onto Harbour Beach on one side and merges into South Beach on the other. It is close to the town and is easy to get to and in the summer you could take a boat trip to Caldey Island from here. Caldey Island is owned and run by an Order of Cistercian monks, who live a simple life farming the island alongside a small village community. They produce quite a few local well known items including chocolate, ice cream, clotted cream, shortbread and yoghurt, plus perfumes and hand lotions made from wild flowers that grow on the island. South Beach is another long stretch of golden sand and always seemed to be quieter and less commercialised but for some reason we didn't go there much, although I thought it was really nice. Overall we tended to go more often to Saundersfoot probably because it was a little quieter but it was also a lovely big beach, with soft golden sands and very safe. It was also a bit easier to get to and to park and had some good cafes. Mind you, because of mam's picnics we wouldn't need to use them much. On the occasions that we did we would have fish and chips with bread and butter and a cup of tea. Annoyingly they always brought the tea straight away so you had to put the saucer on top to stop it getting too cold before the meal arrived.

One year we went on a holiday to North Wales to stay with my aunt and uncle, which was unusual as they normally came to us. Dad had never driven so far in his life but it was quite an adventure. As we got further north some of the roads seemed pretty tricky to me with sheer drops on one side and steep slopes on the other. I used to cling tightly to the door furthest from the edge as I was very frightened. I was struck by the bleakness of where they lived. It was quite high up in the foothills of Snowdonia, south of Carnarvon. There were sheep everywhere, not just in fields, and you had to watch where you walked due to little piles of 'currents' left everywhere by the sheep. The grass seemed quite poor and there were dry stone walls everywhere. The road where they lived led to a quarry where some the famous blue Caernarvon slates were produced. The coast, nice beaches, Caernarvon and Colwyn Bay were all within easy driving distance and by this time my aunt and uncle had a car so we didn't all have to pile into one. Another car incident happened in a car park at a beach on the Llŷn Peninsula.

Dad was reversing to park the car and mam and Auntie Eluned were in the back of the car looking out of the rear window guiding him. They kept saying keep going, keep going and next thing; he had reversed into a ditch. The women in the back thought that this was hilarious and cackled loudly, but dad definitely didn't see the funny side. Fortunately it wasn't too deep, there was no damage and once the ladies had got out of the car he was able to drive out without too much trouble.

As we got older we went on holiday to North Wales more often and not always to stay with my aunt and uncle. We liked the area around Colwyn Bay and a couple of years we stayed there in a caravan. Lyndon didn't come with us at this time but I continued to do so with mam, dad and Brenda and the Richards family of Wenvoe stayed in an adjoining caravan. One other holiday comes to mind. In our mid teens, Lyndon and his friend Michael Adams, John, Cathy and I stayed in a caravan at Poppit for a week, I think during the summer after Lyndon, John and Michael had done their O levels. This was a major adventure for us, we had never done something like this before and we were really lucky with the weather. There were a few caravans which were a couple of hundred yards away from the most popular part of the beach and away from the car park, shop and café. They were situated on a flat sandy section between the road and the dunes so we virtually had our own private path to the beach through the dunes. They were six berth vans so Cathy had the bedroom at the end and the four boys had to make up their beds in the living area each night. We spent the week sunbathing, usually in private sun traps amongst the dunes, swimming, playing various ball games on the beach, eating and sleeping. Going hungry was not an issue as we were well supplied by our parents and we could all manage fairly basic cooking and making sandwiches and there was a shop and café within easy walking distance.

Another place we used to love to visit, although not exclusively in the summer holidays was a small cottage not far from Ffynone House called Nant Mill where my mother's cousin Patty lived. We drove along the road from Boncath towards Newcaslte Emlyn and after a mile or two turned off this road along a narrow country lane down towards a small valley bottom where the cottage was located. One of the many streams in the area ran through the garden and it had a working water wheel on the stream with which we were fascinated. Patty had a lovely garden full of flowers, fruit and vegetables but the highlight for us was the strawberries. Whenever we went there she had a large bowl of ripe, red, juicy, sweet strawberries soaking in syrup, produced by simply adding a bit of water and sugar to the strawberries and letting them soak overnight. She would dish out a big bowlful each for us and they didn't need anything else, they were perfect. If we visited at other times there would always be sandwiches and home baked cakes for us to enjoy, but nothing beat those home grown strawberries.

Of course there were a lot of days during the summer and other holidays when we wouldn't go anywhere. No problem, there were plenty of things to do and as we got older our bikes played an increasingly more important role in our lives. Bikes meant we could go further afield and bike maintenance was obviously important. Fortunately John Sychpant, like dad, was very good with his hands. We used to get old second hand bikes and take them apart, repair and repaint them. We did hit a few snags but we worked it out or got some help from dad. One problem involved the ball bearings inside the wheel of a bike. We had taken everything apart and ended up with ball bearings all over the floor. Every time we collected them and tried to put them back they would fall out again. The solution, as dad showed us was easy. Smear your fingers in grease and pick up the ball bearings which would stick to the grease then scrape them off into their housing at the centre of the wheel (called the hub) and re-fix the wheel to the bike and hey presto, job done.

****

I can't remember any of us having hobbies as such; there was so much going on in the country that we didn't really have much time unless you regard sport as a hobby. Sport was a big part of our lives and there was a group of us who got involved partly because we lived close together and partly because we were friends in school. This group included myself, Lyndon, John, Tony, John Humphreys who was in the same year as John and Lyndon and who lived not far from Sychpant and Michael Adams who was Lyndon's best friend at primary and secondary school. In the early 1960s, Lyndon organised a football match to be played at Crymmych. We rode our bikes to Boncath railway station and took the Cardi Bach to Crymmych. Only two trains a day made the journey then and we were still playing when we heard the train approaching the station. We sent a boy who wasn't playing to the station to ask if they could wait for us as we hadn't finished the match. Apparently they did wait and sent the boy back to tell us to hurry up! I wonder how many boys aged between ten and thirteen, in fact how many people; can say that the train waited for them. Another time John Humphreys took the lead in organising a cricket match and we asked John Allison if he could make a pitch at Sychpant. He agreed, chose a field, cut the grass for a wicket and painted white lines for the boundary and creases. He also made a scoreboard being particularly good with his hands.

Lyndon's interest in rugby started at quite a young age, I preferred to continue playing Cowboys and Indians! Just before going to secondary school he decided that he was going to become a goal kicker so needed some goal posts. John had spent a lot of time exploring the cwm which started south of Sychpant and ran down to Bridell and suggested that it contained plenty of straight timber which would do the trick. They needed to be at least fifteen feet high with a crossbar about eight feet long. So John and Lyndon took an axe and saw on their bikes to search for some suitable trees. They found them easily and brought them back tied between two bikes. This was probably a three mile trip so it was quite an effort. The posts were then placed at the foot of the quarry in front of the rhododendron bushes. This allowed Lyndon to practice from as far as forty yards away, although mostly in front of the posts. Later on a set of posts were put up in Ty Newydd in the field which bordered our garden. I can remember digging out the holes for them spending time on our tummies with our arms in the holes trying to loosen and scoop out the soil. We were very lucky that Brynley and Jack didn't mind us using the field. All the practice obviously paid off as he went on to kick goals for school teams, his university team and for Bridgend RFC. He had a willing apprentice who was happy to kick the ball back to him but I had no interest in goal kicking.

I did try my hand at fishing once and seem to remember that John was quite into it and was quite good. My friend Alan Rumble from Boncath was also keen and he encouraged me to get a simple rod which I did for ten shillings – the same price as my first bike. We once agreed to meet at his house and then go down the road opposite Boncath Main Street, past the post office to a little stream which passed through a mill and was used to drive the mill wheel. To the left of the road the stream ran through a small cwm which Alan visited regularly. We left our bikes by the bridge and walked through the cwm to a pool which was supposed to be good for trout. After a couple of hours Alan caught one small trout but I had no luck. I think perhaps that the way I put the worm on the hook wasn't very effective as whenever I reeled it in the worm was gone but there was no fish. I just stuck the hook once through the worm but apparently it is more effective if you thread the worm over the hook so it can't escape or come free in the flow of water. I think the truth was that I probably didn't have the determination or patience needed to learn how to fish properly. Another time John, Lyndon and I cycled to Llechryd where the River Teifi was quite wide and deep. John had a good rod and I had my ten shilling one with a standard reel without a spinner. A spinner meant you could pull the rod back over your head and in a throwing motion cast the hook and bait into the centre of the river. John was showing us how to pull out the line from my standard reel, then hold it in one hand, and as you whip the rod forward led go of the drawn out line and it had the same effect of casting the hook further into the river, not as effective as a spinner but the next best thing. It does take a bit of practice to get it right and after a few goes Lyndon asked me if he could have a shot. He carefully pulled out the line as John had shown us and whipped the rod forward. Unfortunately he let go of the rod which joined the hook and bait in the river about ten yards away from the bank. John waded in to try and retrieve it but the river soon got too deep so there was no way of getting it back. We could swim a bit but nowhere near well enough to risk going in after it. So that was the end of my dabble with fishing.

Of course accidents were all part of growing up and I can remember being knocked out twice when I was quite young and Lyndon once when he fell down the stairs at my uncle and auntie's house in North Wales when we were on holiday there. My first time was when I was about ten or eleven. The piece of wood running along the top of the kitchen door frame was fairly wide and I used to like to swing on it. One day my grip slipped and I remember waking up in bed about two hours later having, much to my annoyance missed the Wales versus England rugby match which was on television. I was told that I hadn't missed much as it was a low scoring draw with no tries. The second time, I fell out of the door of the school bus. Fortunately it was moving fairly slowly as it was about to stop at Rhoshill for us to get out. I was leaning against the sliding door when someone decided to open it. The next thing I remember was waking up at home, one of my teachers who was following behind the bus had driven me up the road to Brynislwyn and I was again put in bed. Whether it caused any permanent damage is for others to decide. Once when my brother was pushing my sister on the swing, I ran down from the direction of the chicken run and failed to stop in time before crashing into him. Unfortunately the swing was just returning to its highest point and it hit Lyndon just above the eye which was badly cut and swollen and for several days he sported quite a black eye.

Primary School Days

The local school was about two miles away in the village of Blaenffos. Getting to it involved a walk of about a mile down to Rhoshill and up Windy Hill, as far as the left turn to Boncath, where we were picked up by the school transport. This was basically a van with a sliding door and wooden benches fixed to the floor either side which could accommodate eight to ten children. The driver took a circular route via Boncath which enabled him to pick up all the children. The school opened in 1879 and closed in 2004 when the twenty-eight pupils transferred to Ysgol Y Frenni Community Primary School which was newly built alongside the Secondary school in Crymmych and which also accommodated pupils from Crymmych and Hermon Primaries which were also closed. The Blaenffos School buildings were converted to domestic dwellings in 2012/13. Blaenffos is a small village on the A478 Tenby road about half way between Rhoshill and Crymmych. In the 1950s, the first building you came to from the north was the school. Across the road was a small shop and just beyond this was the local church. The rest of the village was stretched southwards along the road and up the hill towards Crymmych. Apart from one other shop the village comprised entirely of housing and a few farms.

The A478 in this area was at one time part of a drovers' road along which would be driven livestock from Irish and local farms as far as England. To cater for these there may at one time have been five public houses in the village and by 1900 there were definitely three still open for business. The hill running southwards out of the village is called Clover Hill and along here was Clover Hill Farm where Jimmy Edwards Rhiwgoi was born and at one time it comprised of the farmhouse, shop, farm buildings and thirteen acres of land. The village was and still is very much in the heart of a rural, farming area.

The Frenni Fawr, the second highest and most northerly peak of the Preseli Hills, looms over the village. It is 1296 feet high but is not a source of any of the famous blue stones. More than once, the whole school walked to the top of this mountain/ hill which must have been about a two mile hike from the school gate to the peak. It was obviously uphill all the way but downhill on the way back. The hill was covered in heather and we were allowed to run down on the way back to school as long as we waited at the bottom and this inevitably involved several tumbles in the soft heather. Apparently there are the remains of Bronze Age barrows (burial places) on the hill and I can remember seeing circular mounds of packed earth covered in heather.

Blaenffos School showing the gated entrance to the school house located at the back of the school. The pedestrian access is just visible to the left of the picture.

The school building was a long single storey stone structure, although there was access to a large loft which was used for storage and at one time had beds for very young children to sleep in during the day. There was a lean-to kitchen attached at the centre and the building had two entrances. Each entrance had a double door opening onto a short corridor and cloakroom area and one door either side, each one giving access to a classroom. There were three classrooms one at each end of the building and a large double sized one in the middle which could be accessed from both corridors. This central classroom served as a teaching area for the oldest children, an assembly hall and a dining hall. During my time at the school the number of children varied between forty-five and fifty-five, there were three teachers and we were split into three classes each one having two year groups. There were two tarmac yards, one for boys and one for girls. The toilets were at the top end of the yards and when I started each cubicle had a single seat with a big drop beneath, these were known as long drop toilets like the ones at Brydell School. During my primary school years these were replaced by proper flush toilets plus a urinal at the boys' side. A favourite game of the boys was to see who could pee the highest up the wall with the ultimate aim was to hit the ceiling, which one or two, including my brother, were able to do. While the conversion work was being undertaken we had a temporary zinc structure in the little area of wood which was located at the top of the boys' yard. Teachers would be reluctant to let you go to the toilet during lesson times and were also a bit mean when doling out toilet paper. Between the woods and the tarmac yard there was an area of dry dirt which contained a large metal climbing frame. At one end of the building there was access behind the building to the school house where the head-teacher lived with his family. This was mostly out of bounds for the children.

Primary school years were mostly happy years. I did quite well academically and loved the fact that we had PE lessons which involved lots of running, football and cricket. The headmaster seemed middle aged, he was tall athletic and had grey hair. He was a very good footballer, well he certainly was compared to the children, and he would always join in the matches. I can remember once in my final year during a match he had a heavy fall on the tarmac yard and had a very nasty graze on his arm. I suppose it shows he was only human as the kids used to have regular falls. I thought he was great and was a significant influence on my life.

The main game in the summer was cricket but we also played rounders. There were usually less than ten boys in the two year groups so just right for two teams allowing everyone to get heavily involved. The yard was a decent size, you got four runs if you hit the walls on either side and six and out if you hit it over the wall. Collecting the ball from the girls' yard was easy enough but retrieving it the other side involved a climb over the wall and a search in a field which was quite rough and had a lot of thistles and a ditch close to the wall which was usually full of nettles. During the summer we would also do some athletics and every year the school sports would be held at a field on the opposite side of the road. During the last two years at school you might be selected to take part in the inter school sports which would take place on the fields of Preseli Secondary School in Crymmych. I remember being very disappointed in my last but one year at school not being selected to represent the school in the sprint race, my brother and his friend Michael Adams had been chosen. I thought I was just as fast and managed to persuade the head to hold a heat during sports day. As the race reached half way Lyndon and Michael were slightly ahead of me but, in an extra effort to stay in touch, I managed to trip on the uneven ground and ended up flat on the floor and in tears of disappointment and anger because, to be honest I knew that I was not fast enough, fall or not. Needless to say I was not selected but fortunately I had another chance the following year and this time was chosen.

The head was also an excellent artist and specialised in oil painting. His portraits of individuals were very realistic and I still have a picture of myself aged about ten or eleven at home. He also painted scenes from school and in particular the local church, identifying quite clearly the various members of the congregation. I was never very good at art and I only once ever did a painting that was good enough to go on the wall. This was basically several streets of houses with smoking chimneys, not quite up to the standard of Lowry, but I suppose the detail and accurate perspective appealed to the head. My favourite subject, which I did quite a few paintings of, was a river running under a stone bridge with fields all round and mountains in the distance - we have something similar in the dining room today but I don't think it's as good as my efforts!

Apart from the head I can remember very well one other teacher at school. She taught us during the first two years. There were about eighteen of us in the class spread across two year groups. Nesta George was young and kind but could be strict if need be. She was short with a full figure, curly hair and glasses. I also have a vague recollection of Mrs. Vine, who, I think, was a temporary teacher, but I remember her very well in secondary school as I always seemed to be in trouble with her. From what I remember I don't think our education was that much different to what is taught now. I suppose the methods might be different, the furniture was older but we were taught in groups in the first two years and then in more formal rows in the following four years. I am pretty sure we were taught all the subjects that my grandchildren are being taught today although they tended to be taught separately then rather than through topics or themes favoured these days. We had sport and a bit of music as the school had a few, mostly percussion, instruments and we did plenty of singing. There was no opportunity for peripatetic music lessons – thank heavens! – piano lessons were enough. In our final year we prepared for the eleven plus and when the time came we had to do examinations in General English, Arithmetic and General Intelligence/Knowledge as well as having to write an essay. A new secondary school, Preseli County Secondary had opened nearby in

1958 and it took all pupils in the area regardless of eleven plus results. However these results were used to determine which class you ended up in. I'm pleased to say that I passed.

Some of the youngest children (roughly half the class) during our first two years, in our classroom, with our teacher Nesta George.

During our final two years we were in the head-teacher's class and, at lunchtime, we had the privilege of going down to the local shop which was just fifty yards away from the school gate but involved crossing the road, not that it was particularly busy. Mam would give us some money to spend and of course we had our pocket money and other 'earnings'. I think my favourite purchases were flying saucer shaped sherbet sweets, lucky bags and love hearts. Although defence spending was cut back during the 1950s there was still a substantial army presence in the UK (both British and USA personnel) and one summer, while at school, we were told that a convoy of soldiers and trucks were going to be passing that day. We all got out in the yard and as many of us as possible climbed onto the wall next to the road. Quite a large convoy of vehicles carrying soldiers and equipment went past and we all cheered as loudly as we could and were rewarded with waves and bars of chocolate which came flying over the wall. Something else occurred round about 1959/60 which I can still remember vividly today. We were visited by two Kenyan students, John Kananura and Clement Agbede. I'm not sure how long they stayed; it was at least a fortnight but possibly longer. They spent time in each of the classrooms and even taught us and it was especially interesting to hear about their home country. They were always cheerful and laughing and would join in with us during sports lessons and in the yards at playtime. Once they played cricket with us but didn't have much of a clue. One of them would spin around; swinging the bat as we bowled, but would inevitably hit the ball during the spin.

The dining area of the large room was at one end and consisted of tables laid in three long rows. As we sat, a bit of a game was to check for a 'llwy two'. The llwy or spoon had either one or two lines of writing on the back of the handle and the first to be seated would look quickly at the back of as many spoons as possible and make sure they had a 'llwy two' – one with two lines of writing. It involved a fairly friendly rivalry (I think), well I can't remember any fights breaking out. Everyone ate at the same time and the supervisors insisted that we eat all the food put in front of us. We weren't allowed to leave the table until everyone had finished. I think that mostly the food was fine; I certainly can't remember any major battles about refusing to eat anything! This part of the classroom would also double up as the stage area for assemblies and concerts. We would have a Christmas Concert and celebrate St David's day much as schools do now. The school also hosted the occasional mini evening concert, a bit like Britain's Got Talent, and one year my brother and I performed the little number 'There's a hole in my bucket', he was Henry and I was Lisa.

Church, Sunday School and the Cardi Bach

We went to church on most Sundays. It was located in Blaenffos, just down the road from the school. Around about 1748 people started to meet in private houses and this went on for many years before the first purpose built church was completed in 1784 and the first service was held there in 1785. It was believed that the first communion service was held in 1787 and the first to be baptised was a lad called David Thomas. In July 1803 John Morgan was ordained as minister and between 1805 and 1806 over one hundred were baptised. As the congregation grew the church was expanded and then replaced in 1807, at a cost of £270, by a building which could accommodate 203 members and replaced again in 1856 by what has become the existing building. Obviously it has been refurbished and updated several times since then. There always seemed to be an appeal for funds, materials and volunteers and members who had particular skills would donate their time to help with repairs and restoration. The church had, and still has, quite a big car park, a good sized vestry and a large well kept graveyard as well as its own outside baptismal pool located between the church and the vestry. The original pool was replaced by a new one which was first used in August 1962 when Wendy Lewis (as it happens, the daughter of one of my dad's cousins) was the first to be baptised along with three other boys from the parish. The church congregation is today much smaller and the local minister, is responsible for four churches known as **Eglwysi Bedyddwyr Cylch y Frenni** (The Baptist Churches of the Frenni Area), holding services in each one of the four churches in turn. Young children went to Sunday school in the vestry while their parents and other adults attended the full service in the church. Communion was given once a month. As you got older you would attend the full service with the adults and there were often services when the children of all ages would get involved. At a certain age children would be baptised. You had to dress in a white shirt and grey trousers or skirt with a belt.

Blaenffos Baptist Church with the baptismal pool in front and the manse to the right (where the minister used to live).

The ceremony took place outside once a year, luckily, usually in the summer. The minister stood in the outdoor pool and the water was really cold. You had to walk down the steps into the pool, the minister grabbed your collar and belt and leaned you backwards into the water until you were completely submerged, and said in Welsh **'Rwy'n eich bedyddio yn enw'r Tad, a'r Mab a'r Ysbryd Glan'** ('I baptise you in the name of the Father and of the Son and of the Holy Spirit') and then lifted you back up. The minister at this time was the Reverend William Jones, a fairly serious traditional preacher who served from 1958 until his retirement in 1988 and I can vividly remember him conducting Brenda's wedding in 1984. Lyndon was baptised in 1965, myself in 1967 and Brenda in 1975. I was quite surprised by these dates as I had the impression that we were younger. Once you were baptised you got to have communion with the grownups.

© Crown Copyright: Royal Commission on the Ancient and Historical Monuments of Wales

© Hawlfraint y Goron: Comisiwn Brenhinol Henebion Cymru

The picture is of the baptismal pool viewed from the church with the vestry in the background

Blaenffos church had its first electric organ in 1961. Before that the organist had to play a harmonium which involved pedalling furiously on the two pedals which were attached to the bottom front of the organ. The electric organ made life a lot easier for the organist but for some years the church has boasted a very impressive pipe organ which requires the organist to use both hands and feet to produce the music a feat which is, I think, as impressive as the looks of the instrument.

There were three other events linked with church which stood out for me. The most memorable was probably the Christmas Party which was held in the vestry every year. All the children and parents were invited; the hall was full to the brim and fully decorated with a big Christmas tree and other traditional decorations. Parents brought cakes and sandwiches - my favourite cake being Madeleines – cone shaped, covered in jam and coconut with a cherry on top. The party culminated in the arrival of **Sion Corn** (Father Christmas.) When most of the lights were turned off we all started singing a Welsh song asking 'who is coming quietly over the hill with his full beard and white hair and something in his sack, who is sitting on the roof next to the big chimney' and culminating in 'Father Christmas, Father Christmas, hello, hello, come here, come on down' (off the roof).

Pwy sy'n dwad dros y bryn, yn ddistaw ddistaw bach

A'i farf yn llais, a'i wallt yn wyn

A rhywbeth yn ei sach

A pwy sy'n eistedd ar y to, ar bwys y simne fawr

Sion Corn, Sion Corn, helo, helo,

Tyrd yma, tyrd i lawr.

Then it all went quiet and the door slowly opened and there he was, in all his splendour and he had a present for everyone.

The second event was what was known as **Pwnc**. In English this means subject or theme. The **Gymanfa Bwnc** as it is called in Welsh has always been held on Whit Sunday (the seventh Sunday following Easter Sunday). Once a year local Baptist churches would gather together to discuss a section from the bible. Children would learn poems and songs and on **pwnc** day we would dress in our Sunday best and sing, recite the poems and answer questions about the chosen bible section. We had obviously studied and been prepared for this in the vestry by the adults running Sunday school. The first **Gymanfa Bwnc** was held in Penuel Baptist Chapel, Cilgerran on the seventeenth of May 1880, with members and children from Blaenffos, Cilfowyr, Penuel and Star taking part. Today, members and children from Bethabara, Blaenffos, Penybryn, Seion Crymmych and Star take part.

The third event was the **Gymanfa Ganu** or Singing Festival which has since 1980 been held during the early May bank holiday. Before then it was held in June or sometimes in April. Up to eight churches were involved (fewer today as some churches have closed). An organising committee with representatives from each church, together with a secretary and treasurer, was established to make the arrangements. The committee chose which hymns to sing and rehearsals were held in the months leading up to the festival. A guest conductor would be invited to run through the final rehearsal on Sunday before the main event on the Bank Holiday Monday. On Sunday the children would perform in the afternoon and the adults in the evening. On Monday the event ran for the whole day, children in the morning, adults in the afternoon and a grand feast of singing in the evening. Food would be provided in the vestry between each session on both days. The festival in Blaenffos was considered to be one of the best in the area and a professional recording company (in the last fifteen to twenty years it's been a local business called 'Cwmni Parrog') would often record the Monday evening session for the radio programme called "**Caniadaeth y Cysegr**" which roughly

114

translated means "singing to a sanctuary"

****

The railway line, known as the Cardi Bach refers to the Whitland and Cardigan Railway, the first part of which, from Whitland to Crymmych, was opened in 1873. At this time there was a road connection (the drovers' road) from Crymmych to Cardigan but it was quite poor. The extension to Cardigan was opened in 1886 and passed through Blaenffos and near Rhoshill with stations at Boncath, Cilgerran and Cardigan. Overall the line was just over twenty-seven miles long. The first section from Crymmych to Whitland followed the valley of the River Taf whose source is in the Preseli Hills, near Crymmych and which flows into Carmarthen Bay near Laugharne. The line was first used to carry lead and silver, which were mined near Llanfyrnach, and slate from quarries in Glogue located to the east of Crymmych alongside the River Taf. These were taken to ports on Carmarthen Bay and later to the port of Cardigan. There was also a passenger service with a train running four times each way per day (later reduced to twice) with an extra service on Saturday and on the day of the monthly agricultural fair at Crymmych.

We knew Boncath station quite well as we would drive over the level crossing on our way to and from school. One of my best friends, Alan Rumble lived in one of the council houses which bordered onto the line and his father and brother had a garage right next to the crossing. We would also visit Cilgerran regularly and would go and see the trains at the station if we were lucky with our timing. It was amazing to see these huge, noisy machines belching smoke out as they chuffed along on the track. Of course my uncle worked in Cardigan station and this one seemed larger than the others, which it probably was, being at the end of the line. We would visit him there sometimes but it wasn't encouraged. The Cardi Bach was closed to passenger trains in September 1962 and completely shut in May 1963 and the entire track was lifted by 1964.

Boncath was and still is quite a small village. In the 1950s the first building that you saw on entering the village was the garage already mentioned, then you crossed the railway line at the level crossing and entered the main street with mostly houses on both sides before coming to a cross roads. There was a public house on the corner on one side of the road and a grocery shop on the other corner. This shop used to sell a range of sweets which were displayed in large glass jars. The owner would weigh out your requirements – usually two ounces or if you were lucky a quarter (four ounces) and put them in a paper bag. If the weight was slightly over he would cut up a sweet to get it just right, sometimes with his teeth, yet he would quite happily offer children a sweet to try, my favourite were pear drops although they were prone to cutting your tongue. By going straight on over the crossroads you could get to Carmarthen via one of the many cross country options, left took you towards Newcastle Emlyn and right would take you to Crymmych. There was also a Post Office and a petrol station on this cross roads. The Newcastle Emlyn to Crymmych road had several more houses in either direction from the cross roads plus the small village hall where I won the recitation competition. Today there are a few more houses and the shop is still there doing a thriving business but the other businesses have gone. The station has gone and the yard is now derelict although for some years it was used as a timber yard.

Crymmych owed its development to the Cardi Bach. Before the railway came only the Crymmych Arms was in existence, probably because it was on the drovers' route. However the community grew quickly and the village became a transport centre and a lot of businesses grew up to service the surrounding agricultural area. It had two churches, a large Co-operative, a village hall and several other shops including general stores, butchers, bakers and later garages and a petrol station. Crymmych soon developed a reputation as the "Wild West of West Wales". No wonder the secondary school had such a good rugby team. The village however, didn't get its own rugby club until 1984. Even though the railway closed in 1964,

Crymmych continued to thrive as an important centre for the agricultural area and later for the tourist industry.

Sport and Entertainment

Sport was a big part of our lives and there was a group of us who got involved partly because we lived close together and partly because we were friends in school. This group included myself, Lyndon, John, Tony, John Humphreys who was in the same year as John and Lyndon and who lived not far from Sychpant and Michael Adams who was Lyndon's best friend at primary and secondary school. In the early 1960s Lyndon organised a football match to be played at Crymmych. We rode our bikes to Boncath railway station and took the Cardi Bach to Crymmych. At that time only two trains a day made the journey and we were still playing when we heard the train that we planned to catch, approaching the station. We sent a boy, who wasn't playing, to the station to ask if they could wait for us as we hadn't finished the match. Apparently they did wait and sent the boy back to tell us to hurry up! I wonder how many boys aged between ten and thirteen, in fact how many people; can say that the train waited for them. Another time John Humphreys took the lead in organising a cricket match and we asked John if he could make a pitch at Sychpant. He agreed, chose a field, cut the grass for a wicket and painted white lines for the boundary and creases and also made a scoreboard.

Lyndon's interest in rugby started at quite a young age, I preferred to continue playing Cowboys and Indians. Just before going to secondary school he decided that he was going to become a goal kicker so needed some goal posts. John had spent a lot of time exploring the cwm which started south of Sychpant and ran down to Bridell and suggested that it contained plenty of straight timber which would do the trick. They needed to be at least fifteen feet high with a crossbar about eight feet long. So John and Lyndon took an axe and saw on their bikes to search for some suitable pieces. They found them easily and brought them back tied between two bikes. This was probably a three mile trip so it was quite an effort and achievement. The posts were then placed at the foot of the quarry in front of the rhododendron bushes. This allowed Lyndon to practice from as far as forty yards away, although mostly in front of the posts. Later on we put up a set of posts in Ty Newydd in the small field which bordered our garden. We had to firstly dig out the holes for them and as the holes got deeper and narrower we had to spend time on our tummies with our arms in the holes trying to loosen and scoop out the soil. We were very lucky that Brynley and Jack didn't mind us using the field. All the practice obviously paid off as Lyndon went on to kick goals for school teams, his university team and for Bridgend RFC. He had a willing apprentice who was happy to kick the ball back to him but I had no interest in goal kicking.

Of course accidents were all part of growing up and I can remember being knocked out twice when I was quite young and Lyndon was knocked out once when he fell down the stairs at my uncle and auntie's house in North Wales when we were on holiday there. My first time was when I was about ten or eleven. The piece of wood running along the top of the kitchen door frame was fairly wide and I used to like to swing on it. One day my grip slipped and I remember waking up in bed about two hours later having missed the Wales rugby match which was on television. It was probably in 1961 when Wales beat England 6 -3 as they said that I hadn't missed much. The second time, I fell out of the door of the school bus. Fortunately it was moving fairly slowly as it was about to stop at Rhoshill for us to get out. I was leaning against the sliding door when someone decided to open it. Next thing I woke up at home, one of my teachers, who was following behind the bus, had driven me up the road and I was again put in bed. Whether it caused any permanent damage is for others to decide. Once when my brother was pushing my sister on the swing, I ran down from the direction of the chicken run and failed to stop in time before crashing into him. Unfortunately the swing was just returning to its highest point and it hit Lyndon just above the eye which was badly cut and swollen but fortunately not bad enough for a visit to the hospital and for several days after he sported quite a black eye.

****

Another source of entertainment was the cinema in Cardigan. Dad mostly used to take us to see the films, the Carry On Films stands out and I seem to remember I thought Carry on Constable was particularly funny. Of course we were too young to get many of the double entendres but much of it was quite slapstick and I remember one scene with several naked police bottoms running across the screen which ten and eleven year old boys would find very rude and therefore funny. The film that stood out for me most of all, I think, was The Ten Commandments, directed by Cecil B. DeMille with Charlton Heston as Moses and Yul Brynner as Ramses. It was released in 1956 so we probably saw it in 1956 or 1957. It was certainly a spectacular film but I was scared to death for much of the time despite it having a U classification. How I managed to last the whole three and a half hours plus I will never know, afterwards I must have had nightmares for days. The scenes of the ten plagues, the parting of the Red Sea and then the drowning Ramses's soldiers as the waves were released and throwing the tablets with the Ten Commandments written on them onto the golden calf were particularly frightening. However I thought the worst scene was when they were building an obelisk and one of the slaves was trapped between two huge blocks of stone as they were being pushed together. Fortunately Moses, who was in charge of the building, did stop the work in time to stop the old woman being crushed. As we got older the cinema would be a good place to go with friends or take a girlfriend on a Saturday night. It was a short walk past the fair field to Finch Square to catch the last bus home. The bus service was provided by the local company Midway Motors who also provided our school transport, so we got to know the drivers quite well, Dai Bach in particular was quite a character. We would get off at Rhoshill and if I was on my own, the walk up the hill in the pitch black was quite scary with lots of strange noises and shadows, so although I say walk, it would usually be a record sprint up the road and a breathless arrival at Brynislwyn.

Many villages held dances and we would go to Cilgerran and Crymmych quite often and there was always a live group and a dance at The Black Lion in Cardigan on a Saturday night. As already mentioned, there would inevitably be a fight sometime during the evening and once my brother was involved in one of these. I've no idea how it started but there were no bouncers and the fight came to the end of its own accord with honours fairly even but with my brother left shirtless. Once when I was about fourteen or fifteen, after going to the cinema, I decided to stay on the bus at Rhoshill and got off at Crymmych where there was a dance. I don't know what I was thinking as I had no way of getting home but I had a date! Fortunately Cathy Allison and her boyfriend Beyron (later to become her husband) saw me and offered me a lift home in Beyron's Land Rover. I asked him to drop me off at Ty Newydd because I didn't want my mother to hear the car stop and start again at our house. I'm sure she would have heard me come in but she never mentioned anything the day after. These dances would often feature local groups and one such group was made up of pupils from my secondary school, Preseli. This included my friend Alan Rumble and my brother's friend John Humphreys and they were really quite good. I was very envious of and impressed with my friend Alan as I thought he was a great guitarist. In the mid to late 1960s being in a pop group was quite the thing, with teenagers emulating their heroes like the Beatles, The Rolling Stones, The Who, The Hollies, Cream (featuring Eric Clapton) and for the guitarists Jimmy Hendrix as well as Eric Clapton and George Harrison.

The Big Freeze and Snow of 1963

This actually started on the twenty-seventh of December 1962, the day that Jean and Mary went over the hedge on the sledge. The weather wasn't bad enough to prevent us from collecting **calennig** on the first of January but soon got much worse. It continued into the third week of February with brief daytime thaws but freezing nights with further snowfalls and blizzards. From the thirtieth of December it became very windy with more snow and freezing temperatures and within a few days there was deep snow on the ground. The freezing wind caused large snow drifts that were great for sledging off. The start of my second term at the Secondary School was quite disrupted, we could walk down to Rhoshill often over deep drifts but the bus didn't always come. When we did get to school we didn't get much work done, examinations were postponed and on many days we were sent home early.

Most children love snow and we were no exception. While it was tough going for our parents it was paradise for us, we did a lot of sledging and exploring of snow drifts. There were power cuts and frozen pipes to deal with. At one time when Rhiwgoi's pipes were frozen Brynley and Jack supplied them with water in churns as the spring at Wenvoe was still pumping water but at another time it was their turn to suffer frozen pipes and they were able to access water from us using a long hosepipe and churns. Power cuts meant we had to use oil lamps. We still had two or three working lamps - the brass version with a wick and glass chimney. Despite the cold weather, sitting in the kitchen with a roaring fire and a couple of oil lamps was quite cosy but bed time wasn't quite as much fun especially in my cold room with a layer of ice on the single glazed window. I wonder if that made it double glazing?!

There was no problem with fuel for the lamp, we were able to use diesel from a large tank at Wenvoe. Once I volunteered to get some more from the shed where the tank was located. It was very cold, dark and there was a blizzard blowing but hey-ho, it was an adventure. I walked around our house, down the steps, up the road to the main farm gate by the milk stand. The zinc shed was just inside the gate and I managed to get the large zinc door open but I couldn't figure out how to operate the tap. By now I was getting really cold and it was no longer and adventure so I kicked the tap and the diesel came flowing out onto the snow so I quickly put the jug under the tap until it was full. By the time I got home I was frozen, my hands and feet were numb and I was in tears. Then I couldn't remember if I had managed to turn the tap off so mam had to wrap up and go over to check. Luckily I had somehow managed but had no memory of how I had done it - perhaps another kick. I don't remember where dad was but I expect he was at work although I doubt that they would be firing many missiles.

While the main road was kept relatively clear the road up from Rhoshill past Brynislwyn to Sychpant soon became impassable. There was a severe blizzard in early February with drifts up to fifteen feet deep. I remember Brynley standing on top of a drift on the road between Wenvoe and Sychpant and being able to touch the telegraph wires. As early as the fourth of January Gordon and Margaret Sychpant had to drive their tractor with a link box on the back along the road to Rhoshill and into Cardigan to get vital supplies. After the blizzard of early February he had to again use his tractor but this time it had a scoop attached to the front which helped to clear a path through to Wenvoe and then he helped Jack and Brynley knock through one of their field's hedges thereby allowing them to get their milk down to the main road as the milk lorry couldn't get up the road from Rhoshill. Around this time Gordon and Margaret also drove the tractor across fields southwards from Sychpant past Penlanbridell towards the Eglwyswrw to Boncath road which wasn't as blocked. They also managed to get to the main road at Rhoshill and down to Trip Farm where they borrowed Dan's van to go into Cardigan, again for supplies. In early February the Allisons started digging sheep out of drifts following the blizzard and continued to do so for several days. They were able to locate them by searching for the air holes their breaths had made in the compacted snow. As they dug down they found that the warmth of the sheep's body had created a cocoon around them (well they did have thick sheepskin coats) and though hungry they were none the worse for their ordeal. When the snow thawed virtually all the fences needed repairing as the wires had been damaged due to the pressure from the weight of the snow. Also on the fifth of February the postman had gamely struggled as far as Sychpant where Gordon and Margaret advised him not to venture on. He decided to continue, only to eventually give up and return to stay the night at Sychpant. Although the snow was still deep, the blizzard had passed by the following day, so he was able to continue on after one night of the Allison's hospitality.

Eventually by mid February Gordon finished digging through the snow as far as Wenvoe but unfortunately he became seriously ill and by the start of April was admitted to Glangwili Hospital in Carmarthen where he stayed for a month. Fortunately Margaret was able to visit him nearly most days thanks to friends and neighbours who drove her there. I have to say that in that respect things haven't changed much as my parents today can rely on friends and neighbours for visits to the doctor, hospital and shops. During the time that Gordon was ill Cathy stayed home from school to help her mother on the farm. While the road from Wenvoe past our house as far as the entrance to Ty Newydd was reasonably clear, there were deep drifts down the hill past Rhiwgoi towards Rhoshill. The four families all pitched in to help clear a single track through the drifts and the kids did their bit with shovels. Eventually we were able to get a tractor down as far as Dan Trip's field and through there to his farm and the main road. I can remember for days walking down the road with a wall of snow on our right hand side where the drifts were deepest and it took several weeks for this to disappear completely.

My recollections of the snow of 1963 were of fun and excitement but of course it was far more serious for the grownups. However my father says that this was nothing compared to the winter of 1947. Despite an unseasonably mild early part to the winter January, February and March brought heavy snows and severe cold with drifts even higher than 1963 and low temperatures for several weeks, even the River Thames was frozen, five metre drifts were not uncommon. There were power cuts and shortages of food and the army was deployed to help areas which were particularly hard hit. During the first day of heavy snow dad was working in Pantyderi farm until late in the evening and then had to make his way home to Cilwendeg Lodge where he was staying with his brother and sister in law Emlyn and Elsie. He somehow managed to get his motorbike home but the following day he was expected at work and took his pushbike, but eventually had to walk to and from work, a journey of over four miles each way. No offer of board and lodge was forthcoming which I thought was a bit mean.

Secondary School Days

Ysgol Y Preseli

I started at Ysgol Y Preseli Secondary School in September 1962 dressed in a maroon blazer, grey trousers and cap which had to be bought from a specialist supplier in Cardigan. It was a new school opened in September 1958 so the first intake would have been in year eleven by the time I started (it was called form five then). Up to then pupils from North Pembrokeshire attended grammar or secondary modern schools in Cardigan or Narberth. Comprehensive schools didn't open in Wales until 1964 but Preseli took all pupils in the area so resembled a comprehensive – trailblazers from the start! We had to sit the eleven-plus and the result determined which class you were placed in. Preseli had four classes per year plus a few children in a Special Needs class. If you passed your eleven-plus you were placed either in a class taught through the medium of Welsh or one taught through the medium of English, each class had between twenty and thirty pupils. I was initially placed in the Welsh Medium class but after a week I asked to be transferred because, although Welsh was my first language, I was struggling with being taught all the subjects in the Welsh Language. When I stepped into the new class for the first time I'll never forget being greeted by Neville Boulton who said 'Hey man, can you do the twist' and proceeded to show me how it was done. I hadn't come across the twist before but I felt right at home thanks to that welcome. The school went fully bilingual in 1991 and is now classified as a category 2A bilingual school which means that most stuff is done in Welsh.

The school offered a good mix of subjects. During the first three years (now known as key stage three) we studied English, Welsh, French, Latin, Biology, Chemistry, Physics, Arithmetic, Algebra, Geometry, Geography, History, Art, RE, Woodwork and Metalwork for the boys and Needlework and Cookery for the girls plus PE and Games. Over the next two years (key stage four) most of these subjects were offered at O level and a new subject, Economics was added. I studied English Language and Literature, Welsh Language and Literature, Double Mathematics (all of which were compulsory), Latin (you had to have a Language), Biology (you had to have a Science), Geography and Economics all of which I managed to pass although I had to have two goes at Latin. One of my year group and friend Martin Lloyd was appointed Head in 1991 and during his almost eighteen years in charge, was largely responsible for transforming the school's profile and success as measured in pupil numbers, examination results and Inspection Reports (despite a shaky start with falling numbers for some time). He was aided and abetted for some of this time by Cerwyn Davies, who was Chair of Governors, another friend from the same year group who continues to farm locally. Before being appointed Head, from around 1977 Martin was Economics teacher at the school, following in the footsteps of one of my favourite teachers Des Jones. Being an

Economics teacher myself I considered applying for the job but it was just as well I didn't as it would have been a waste of time. The school was made up of a mixture of·single and two storey blocks linked together around a central tower of four floors. Two of the floors of the tower had four classrooms each; one level housed the Art room (double sized) and two classrooms while the ground floor contained the library and one classroom, mostly used for Sixth Form lessons. Even though it was quite new it was soon extended with the typical prefabricated buildings commonly seen in schools. By today the school buildings have expanded considerably with new 'permanent' blocks including a swimming pool and sports centre plus a block housing the Sixth Form. It has become an important community facility and the school hall doubles up as a Community Theatre.

As with my primary education, I have many happy memories of my time at Ysgol Y Preseli, even though I was in trouble quite a bit. Looking back now I think that I was probably a bit of a bully in my early years, although being small, (I was five foot nothing when I entered the Sixth Form) I never picked a fight with anyone smaller than me. I was summoned to the Head, W R Jones (commonly known as Bwff - no idea why) quite early in my first year. I had been sticking a pin into the leg of another boy on the school bus – hence the summons to the Headmaster's room. As I entered he was stood behind his desk in his gown, flexing a bamboo cane and his first words were 'have you ever had the cane boy'. I was never called to see him again while he was in post. My fear was evidently short lived as I was soon in trouble again. At the end of break we would sometimes sneak in to the toilets to grab a drink from the cold water fountain, this one time there was a bit of a queue so I pushed to the front and hit the boy who protested. I went to my class and was immediately called to see Mrs Vine who managed quite easily to reduce me to tears. As the snow of 1962/63 was slow to clear we still had quite a bit on the school grounds so playing snowballs was quite common. While taking part in this 'pastime' a boy ran up to me from behind and dropped a big lump of snow on my head. I was naturally unhappy about this so chased him and tripped him up so he went flying into the slushy mud. I couldn't understand why a small group of girls from my class were cross with me for what I did!

There were two boys with whom I had running battles during my first couple of years in school. One of them arrived at the start of the second year and being captain of the rugby team I felt I had a certain position to maintain amongst the boys in my year group. The new boy was about the same size as me and was also a good rugby player so was seen as a rival and it didn't take much encouragement from my friends to suggest that he might be a threat to my 'position'. So to some extend we were goaded into having a fight (although it didn't take much goading). This went on for a little while before we developed a respect for each other and became good friends. There was another boy that I had a running battle with, and I have no idea why. It finished when we had a particularly nasty encounter where he butted me in the mouth and loosened and chipped my front tooth - damage which I have to this day. I went after him with tears of anger and pain and after a bit of wrestling I asked him if he had had enough. The fight stopped with, I think, honour intact on both sides. I thought he had given up because he had had enough and he must have thought that I said I had had enough. Again we became good friends. There was one other incident that I felt quite ashamed about. I had been picking on a boy who was in the year below me, he was big and a little overweight and Des Jones got to hear about our altercations so, having a background as a boxer, he arrange for me and the other boy to have it out in the gym with boxing gloves. Four benches were placed in a square to act as a ring and we started a bit of sparring until I caught him with a good hard right to the nose which started bleeding, so I stopped straight away as I felt sorry for him. Again we got on fine after that! Fights were quite common in school then (and I suspect in all schools). When my brother started school he was picked on by a boy in the third year who was part of a bigger group - big mistake – let's just say that after that incident he left my brother alone and some of the group became quite friendly with him.

I think by form three (year nine) I had settled down and controlled my aggression a little better. I certainly don't remember any more incidents until a couple in the Sixth Form. The first involved the then Head James Nicholas. He was a very good mathematician and I think a bit of a philosopher. He used to take us for General Studies which could involve discussion on just about anything and seemed to me to be quite deep (and dry) at the time. These lessons were held in the library and the tables would be set in a square around the edge of the room which meant that we were always facing someone. I was struggling to concentrate and caught the eye of another pupil sitting opposite me and we started to giggle. This went on for a little while until the Head had had enough and suggested I see him in his office after the lesson. There was no major telling off, which I would probably have preferred but a little discussion about my misbehaviour. He seemed satisfied when I told him that I found some of the topics difficult but tried my best and also suggested to him that I was a regular contributor to the discussion which he accepted and seemed happy with. Later in the year we took part in a religious discussion which was recorded for the radio. My contribution, which the head liked, was that I felt that the Old Testament should be treated like the Greek Myths rather than being taken as factually correct.

The second incident involved the Woodwork teacher who was our form teacher and Head of Sixth Form, Mr Harris who was a scary fellow with a head of ginger hair and large beard. The first time I saw him was when we were lining up ready to go into the lesson and he came down the corridor and bawled out 'There's a strong smell of boys here'. I assume he meant sweat as we had just come in from morning break! He registered the Upper Sixth in a small room in one of the prefabricated building which was used mostly as a Sixth Form common room. The room was a little run down and was due for redecoration. That lunch hour someone had been kicking a football against the wall and it had left a lot of imprints on the wall. Mr Harris wasn't happy and demanded to know who the culprits were. I suggested that it might be part of the redecoration. Oops bad timing combined with a lack of a sense of humour meant a visit to his store room for 'a chat'. When dealing with Sixth Formers 'a chat', where we sat opposite each other on stools, was considered more appropriate than a telling off or some sort of punishment, which I would have much preferred.

Although I have highlighted some of the run ins I had with other children and teachers my time at Ysgol Y Preseli was very happy and productive. I worked hard and was supported and encouraged by my parents and teachers and I managed to get good results in both internal and external examinations. Apart from the academic work there were always lots of other things going on, sport being a very important one for me as well as for my brother and sister. Rugby was the big thing and I played for one school team or other for every year I was at school. I got county trials for both under fifteens (as outside half) and senior levels (as a scrum half) and had good games in each. However Glyn Bowen, our History teacher who had taken me and prop Wynford Daniel to the under fifteens trial said that I wasn't picked because they felt I was too small. Having ended the game with concussion and being sick on the way home might have suggested that they had a point. In the senior trial I was told that I was one of the best players on the field but the pupil who was picked in my place had played before and did not take part in the trial as he was injured. I was reserve for all the games and dutifully ran the line but unfortunately did not get a game. It was some consolation that I went on to play for Swansea University for four years being captain for two of them including in my fourth year (my teacher training year) when we reached the Universities Athletic Union final at Twickenham having beaten Durham University in the semi-final. Unfortunately we were stuffed in the final by Loughborough Colleges, which despite being a sports training college, was somehow allowed to play in the competition. It wasn't Fran Cotton or Louis Dick (full internationals even then) who did the damage but a young flyer from Llanelli called Clive Rees, we just had no answer to his pace and elusiveness.

We participated in athletics and cricket in the summer term and the highlight was the school sports. Although I was quick, I wasn't quick enough to represent my house in the sports day sprints, but for some reason, despite my size, I did quite well in the hurdles, my style being jump and run flat out between each hurdle. I was also good at walking and one year I was dawdling around near the hundred yard track when I looked across and saw the walking race starting from the 200 yard start line. I sprinted across the track and asked Glyn Bowen (the starter) if I could go after them and he said yes, so off I went. I don't know if I was cheating but I managed to move pretty fast and, as the race was relatively long, I managed to catch most of the competitors and came in third – a race I should have won if I had been less dozy.

There was a strong cultural tradition in the school and one highlight was the annual St David's Day eisteddfod. As in most schools we were split into houses and competed in both on stage and off stage competitions. In the weeks building up to the eisteddfod each of the subject teachers set competitions at different age levels. Examples of work produced in craft lessons could be entered (cookery was very popular) and other tasks included making models for history, maps for geography and poems and short stories in the languages. I particularly enjoyed making models in History, one year making a working trebuchet (a medieval weapon which is used to catapult heavy stones against a fortified building like a castle) and another year an assault tower. We had to submit our entries with a nickname and one year I chose Mighty Mouse, much to the amusement of many of the staff. I scored a lot of house points that year, both off stage and on stage and for the off stage events you had to stand up when they announced the first, second and third placed so

I stood up a few times that year. On the day before the eisteddfod all the work submitted would be displayed in the gym and parents were invited to visit to see their children's work. We would also learn poems and songs both individually and in groups ready for the on stage competition with one entry chosen to represent each house. One highlight for me during the first three years was being part of the gymnastics display team which performed at the eisteddfod. This involved both floor and apparatus work with a big finish being a vaulting exhibition over the horse with the vaulters crossing at ninety degrees in quick succession which looked very impressive.

As well as sport and the annual eisteddfod there was the Christmas Concert which we were encouraged to participate in. If we weren't good enough for an individual or small group performance many of us joined the school choir all singing soprano or alto in the first few years but then tenor or base as we got older. My Music teacher wanted me to do a solo when I was in the Sixth Form but for me that was one step too far. The Literary and Debating Society was also well attended when we were in the Sixth Form. We would have traditional debates (on the line of 'This house believes') on a range of topical issues with usually two speaking for and two against. Also popular were Balloon Debates which involved the participants playing the role of a well-know individual and making a case for not being thrown out of the balloon. One participant would be eliminated after each round so the final two contestants would have to speak three times. Although I was Chairman of the society I still took part in debates.

I remember several teachers quite well and, like most people who have had teachers that influenced their lives in various ways, I was no exception. As already mentioned one of my favourites was Des Jones, (the Economics teacher with the boxing background), as well as being an inspiring Economics teacher he helped a lot with university applications and probably influenced my decision to teach Economics and go to Swansea where Professor Nevin (the author of the main text book we used) lectured. In the first few years of my career I taught classes in exactly the same way as Des Jones taught us and it was very effective. It was a close run thing however with Tom Geog., Graham Thomas our Geography teacher from the first year to the Sixth Form, who was also great and I did Geography and PE for my Postgraduate Certificate in Education (PGCE). Sport was a big thing for us in school, particularly rugby and I thought the first PE and Games teacher we had was superb. His name was Geoff Reed from Ystalyfera, and, although he moved on when I was in my second or third year, he gave us a terrific grounding in the sport. He once arranged a match against his old school at Ystalyfera and we had chips after the match, unheard of at Preseli. During his time at Preseli school teams rarely lost and I had the 'honour' of captaining the under-thirteen team to their first defeat in 1964! He was also great at teaching gymnastics which I really took to and was one of the first year one pupils to do a flick flack, which is a backward hand spring. A forward hand spring is where you jump forward to land on your hands and immediately flick your legs over to land on your feet, while a flick flack involves you throwing yourself backwards to land on your hands before flicking your legs over to land on your feet. Jones Met (Brian Jones) taught metalwork, I thought he was pretty rough and ready and quite strict but I suppose you had to be in the workshop environment with all the cutting and shaping tools as well as a blacksmith's hearth for young boys to 'play' with. We were allowed to use the hearth after training and with supervision. Mr Jones had a slightly receding hairline and one day while trying to light the hearth he managed to singe the front of his hair which exposed even more of his forehead. He did very well to control himself after that little episode!

The first Head, W R Jones taught us Latin in year one and these lessons were followed by Games. During one lesson it was raining quite hard and Bwff decided that there would be no rugby that afternoon due to the weather, so we had an extra Latin lesson instead. Ten minutes later we could hear the sounds of metal studs on the tarmac yard as the rest of the first year boys went out to the rugby field; I was not a happy bunny. From my second year (1963) I was taught Latin by Geraint Harries Williams and he had a completely different approach to the subject, he made it more fun and more interesting. He was also a very jovial and charismatic individual which helped to endear us to the subject. It is often said that the teacher is more important than the subject and in this case it was certainly true. I still remember quite a bit of the subject and a little verse made entirely of Latin words stands out which looks and sounds like a badly spelt English poem:

Caesar ad sum iam forte, Augustus aderat

Caesar sic in omnibus, Augustus sic in at

Caesar had some jam for tea, Augustus had a rat

Caesar sick in omnibus, Augustus sick in hat.

He was very impressed with a drawing I had done during the O level mock examination of the attacking and defensive lines in some battle that featured in a book we studied by (I think) Virgil and which consisted of a number of circles which he compared to a dart board. Unfortunately it didn't earn me any extra marks. Mr Harries-Williams suffered from some form of disability which meant his legs were very weak and could not support him properly so had to walk with two sticks. However it didn't slow him down nor hinder his sunny outlook and despite this disability he was a sensational table tennis player, he would discard his walking sticks and, with legs splayed out, would dominate one side of the table. He used to supervise us at a Youth Club and taught us how to improve our table tennis game. He may well have taken over teaching us Latin in 1963 because the head teacher, W R Jones retired to be replaced as Head by James Nicholas. When he arrived the school wasn't designated as a specific bilingual school but this was his dream for the school and soon it also became a Community School providing Adult Evening classes and this allowed him to invite prominent local literary individuals like Tecwyn Lloyd and Waldo Williams to lecture there.

Another Jones, this time Aneurin, was our Art teacher and Head of the Art Department from the day the school opened in 1958 until his retirement in 1986. He was quite a talented artist who produced and sold paintings commercially, he tended to specialise in painting people particularly locals from Mid and West Wales, especially farmers, although he also painted buildings and animals, horses being a particular favourite. He regularly exhibited his work at the National Eisteddfod and won the main Art prize in 1981. Reggie Evans (repeating Reggie) was also appointed in 1958 and was a very effective Mathematics teacher, partly due to the fact that he would repeat everything several times but also because he could break the subject down into simple concepts which we could all easily understand. When he gave our books back after marking he would stand at the front of the class and throw them to the pupils. One of our weekly lessons was on the top floor of the tower (the same room where the head taught us Latin) my friend and I, were sat at the back next to the window and so decided to open the window in the hope that the book would duly exit. The book was thrown, I made a feeble attempt to catch it and out of the window it went much to the delight of the whole class. I then had to go down three flights of stairs to retrieve it which wasted a good five minutes.

Glyn Bowen taught History and he was also a good cricketer so would take us for cricket during our summer games lessons. Although he wasn't Head of Department he took us for History at O and A level. I chose History as one of my subjects at A level but after a week or so I felt it wasn't for me so I decided to switch to Mathematics instead. Unfortunately I couldn't fit in the obvious choice of Pure and Applied Mathematics into my timetable so ended up doing Pure Mathematics which was a lot more difficult and I really struggled particularly as the Head, who taught us, and the other three pupils in the class seemed to be natural mathematicians. I was more delighted with the E grade I scraped for this subject than the much better grades I got for Economics and Geography and it did help quite a lot when studying Economics at university. In the short time that I did history we managed to play a trick on Glyn Bowen. Before he arrived for one of the lessons we loosened the joints in his chair (teachers sat on ordinary pupil chairs when teaching in the Sixth Form prefabricated building) so that when he sat on it the chair collapsed and he ended up on the floor. We vehemently denied that we knew anything about the condition of the chair and tried to look concerned whilst stifling the urge to laugh. As he did not have his own teaching room he carried everything around in an old battered suitcase and it always took him a while to look through and find what he needed for our lesson. Once the suitcase was precariously balanced on the desk and ended up on the floor with the contents scattered. At least he had a sense of humour and suggested that it gave him a good opportunity to tidy it up.

We were taught English for most of the first five years by the Deputy Head, Nancy Rees and she could make the subject really interesting. At that time we studied both English Language and English Literature as two separate O level subjects. The textbook used for English Language was, if I remember rightly, called First Aid in English which was full of information about English Grammar, so we knew all about nouns, pronouns, verbs, adverbs, adjectives, active voice and passive voice, prepositions, conjunctions and structure of sentences. I can still remember one particular poem from this book:

The elephant is a bonny bird.

It flits from bough to bough.

It makes its nest in a rhubarb tree

And whistles like a cow.

It's pretty meaningless and is called a nonsense verse but it's full of grammatical rules and obviously easy to remember! We also studied a number of novels but the only two that come to mind are Mill on the Floss and the Moonstone. My favourite part of lessons was when she explained idioms, for example 'a bird in the hand is worth two in the bush', 'a stitch in time saves nine', 'absence makes the heart grow fonder', 'still waters run deep', 'Hobson's choice'. She gave us a list of these to copy into the back of our books with three or four lines left between each one. At the end of most lessons she would spend a few minutes explaining the origin and meaning of one or more of these and we had to write down the explanation in the gaps left as she talked. I have already mentioned Mrs Vine, she had been a Mathematics teacher at the school since it opened and although I was never taught by her I did come across her quite often (and not always because I was in trouble). Although strict and sometimes a bit scary she was hardly ever in a bad mood, mostly very kind and knew all the children well and always made us feel important. As mentioned earlier she also taught in Blaenffos for a while before Preseli opened.

Two of my heroes while I was in my first and second years were sixth formers Selwyn Williams and Arwel Owen partly because they both got selected to play rugby for Wales Senior Schoolboys, Arwel as a wing forward and Selwyn as a scrum half. Some mates and I would regularly wrestle with them in the cloakroom area while they supervised us during wet breaks or dinner hours. Selwyn went on the play for Llanelli RFC for several years and I got the honour of playing against him for Bridgend during the mid 1970s. That was the most incredible experience I had on the rugby pitch, playing in front of a packed crowd under floodlights at Stradey Park with both sides determined to play open rugby. The noise was deafening and unrelenting and it certainly lifted you, I shudder to think what it must be like to play an international match at the Principality Stadium in Cardiff. Many of the Llanelli team that evening had been involved in the memorable defeat of the All Blacks in the fourth match of their tour in October 1972. Selwyn was a substitute for that game as

Raymond 'Chico' Hopkins, who had one Welsh international cap and one Lions cap, was also at the club. Chico Hopkins started his career at Maesteg RFC and after a few years with the Scarlets, moved to rugby league in 1972 so Selwyn got his number one spot back.

I left secondary school in the summer of 1969 bound for Swansea University. My school career spanned a big chunk of the 1960s which many consider to be one of the most important decades of the century. There were certainly many changes in culture and society and I left feeling that I had experienced a fantastic few years which would have been hard to beat though I realised later at university how naïve I still was. By the time we were in the Sixth Form there was a constant battle about hair length with Norman Harries in the forefront of telling the boys to get their hair cut. In 2008 to celebrate the schools fiftieth birthday, Brian Jones (Jones Met.) and Graham Thomas (Tom Geog.) were instrumental in putting together a book called **Atgofion Dysgu Byw** (the school motto was **Cofia Dysgu Byw,** meaning Remember to Learn to Live while **atgofion** means memories). The book is a collection of memories about their time in school by former staff and (mostly well known) former pupils and includes reference to each of the four former Head teachers – W R Jones, James Nicholas, George Ladd and Martin Lloyd as well as the then Chair of Governors Cerwyn Davies. The final contribution to the book is by Michael Davies who took over as head teacher from Martin Lloyd. It has been good to see that Mr Davies has ensured that Preseli has continued to be such a great school and that standards have been kept at such a high level that it has become one of the best secondary schools in Wales. As Lyndon had made a contribution to the book, (I had no idea he could write such fluent Welsh) we went down to West Wales for the launch event and were of course obliged to buy at least one copy each of the book, plus one for mam and dad.

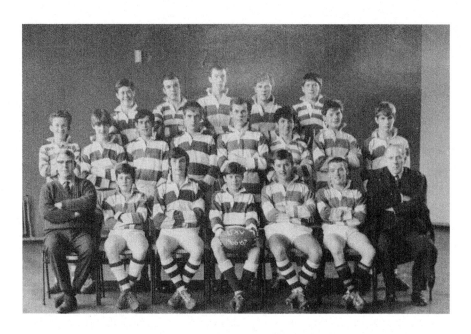

Under 16 Rugby Team 1967

First XV 1969

Transport and Summer Jobs

When I was old enough to drive I decided I would rather have a motor bike than drive a car so dad bought a second hand BSA Bantam. This was a good bike for a beginner, it had a maximum speed of 50 mph (but I never managed to get it to reach that) and was very economical doing up to 150 miles to the gallon. Its two stroke engine ran on petrol but each time you filled it up you had to put a small amount of oil in as well and then give it a good shake to mix it. I could ride the bike with L plates on a provisional licence but decided to do the driving test which involved riding a certain route around Cardigan a few times while the examiner walked on foot, so was only able to observe at certain points. The whole test was conducted at well below the speed limit which was just as well when he stepped out in front of me for the emergency stop. With three questions on the highway code correctly answered I passed on my first attempt. The bike was great to get around on even in the uncertain weather of West Wales but I did have three spills. The first was on an awful night when I was riding back from an evening at the Youth Club in Eglwyswrw. I had turned off the main road from Eglwyswrw onto the country lane leading to Rhoshill. As I was riding along this road, the rain was pelting down, it was pitch black and I was soaking wet but I was taking it carefully. However there was one sharp bend too many and I skidded on the wet road surface and the bike went sliding one way while I went the other way. It was a slow crash with no damage done to myself, the bike seemed undamaged too but I couldn't get it started. Fortunately there was a telephone kiosk a few hundred yards away on a side lane next to a few houses and I was able to call dad who came out in his car. He soon got the bike going and I managed to ride it the remaining couple of miles home.

The second spill was a bit more serious. I was riding to Cardigan to play in a rugby match for Cardigan RFC when, just before Bridell School, a friend went past in the other direction in his father's pick up van so I turned to wave at him and spent a bit too long looking behind me. I ended up in the hedge and as I was doing about 30 mph I hit it quite hard. Fortunately it was a fairly overgrown soil hedge with a few bushes but no trees so it could have been much worse especially as I just missed a gate post. The bike was damaged and I had quite a few bumps and grazes and was a bit shaken. There was a farm track just opposite so I limped down a couple of hundred yards and managed to telephone Brynley who came out with his car and trailer. We put the bike in the back and after a few days dad managed to repair the minor damage it had sustained. Needless to say I wasn't able to play in the rugby match.

During my first year at university I stayed at Neuadd Gilbertson which was based in Clyne Castle, a Grade II listed building located on a hill overlooking Swansea Bay, on the road to Mumbles. I thought it would be quite useful if I had my motorbike with me as the hall of residence was a long walk from the university campus and from the sports ground and pavilion at Sketty Lane where we played rugby and trained. To my surprise dad agreed but would not let me ride it from Brynislwyn to Clyne Castle so, while my mother drove the car, he rode the bike dressed in a long brown coat with a belt around the middle and a flat cap (plus clothes under his coat of course!). It took us a while but we got there safely and fortunately there was a barn at the hall of residence where I could keep it under cover. The road from the hall down to the main Swansea to Mumbles road was a narrow tarmac lane and one frosty morning, on my way to lectures, I was riding gingerly and managed to negotiate the hilly section pretty well but as I approached the main road I braked gently and the bike slowly slid from under me. Fortunately I was going quite slowly and managed to hold onto it with my feet also sliding along the road, it felt like I was on a speedway track, sliding along sideways. The main road had been gritted and was safely negotiated. When I eventually got myself a car dad held onto the bike for several years before selling it to my cousin Leslie and he also kept it for quite a few years as it had become a vintage model.

Dad on the BSA Bantam in fancy dress – his fireman uniform and a police hat - an outfit I was going to wear at Cilgerran Carnival. Alongside we still had my first bike.

My first car was a grey Morris Minor which I bought for £100 from a farmer located near Clunderwen. Dad didn't want me to buy it as the chassis underneath was covered in cow dung accumulated over a lengthy period and he thought the chassis would eventually rust badly. But I was in a hurry to get a car as I needed it to drive from home to Lampeter to continue my summer job labouring for a couple of plasterers, so I didn't listen and bought it. Eventually the floor did need welding but otherwise it was a solid reliable car. It had a sturdy iron trailer hitch on the back which was particularly handy when I reversed into a tree in the driving rain while having to give way to a bus on a narrow street in Swansea. I had a feeling that there might have been something behind as I reversed but wasn't sure until I came to a juddering halt, but there wasn't a scratch on the car – well nothing new anyway. It didn't have electric indicators but small orange arms which came out of the pillar located between the two doors of the car. Unfortunately after giving a friend a lift once I forgot to cancel the indicator and he walked into it and broke it. I managed to repair the arm with some tape but it was a bit of a tight fit in its housing and whenever I turned left I had to lean over behind the passenger and hit the door pillar hard so the indicator would pop out. It was still in the same condition when I sold it to another friend Brian Toms, but he didn't seem to mind. He once drove it through a flooded field at Swansea University grounds and as he continued onwards to join the traffic on the main road he found that the brakes weren't working. Fortunately he managed to negotiate himself into the traffic flow without too much difficulty and he was fine once the brakes had dried out. Apparently the car reached the end of its life when Brian turned it over on Fairwood Common on the Gower Peninsula.

I was eighteen when I tried my driving test, dad had taken me out quite a lot in his car but I had only had a few formal driving lessons. My driving instructor didn't feel I was ready for the test but I had applied and had been given a date so I didn't see the harm in having a go. I had a lesson immediately before the test and mid-way through the lesson my instructor told me to turn right ahead so I did only to find that I was about to drive down a one way street. He had meant for me to turn right at the road junction which was another fifty yards ahead. This convinced him even more that I was not ready and was going to fail. During my test the examiner took me on the same route and told me to turn right ahead so I made sure I didn't make the same mistake twice and just after the no entry road he slammed the dashboard for and emergency stop which I did perfectly! I answered one of the Highway Code questions incorrectly but he asked me again and with a bit of prompting I got it right and by some miracle I passed.

****

After finishing my O levels and for several summers after that while I was in the Sixth Form and at University I had summer jobs which were a very handy source of income and which kept me out of mischief. The first one I had was at Close Farm which I could easily get to on my push bike. The first week was an eye opener. I had to get up at six (unheard of), have mam's breakfast, usually bacon and egg and start work at seven. Then it was breakfast number two at about nine o'clock once milking had finished. Mid morning would be tea and cake followed by lunch just after mid-day. Mid afternoon break would involve another cup of tea and something to eat. Gladys Nicholas who lived in Rhoshill worked at Close and she would be the one dishing out tea and cakes. After finishing my cup of tea she would always pick up the teapot and ask 'Tea?' As I didn't like to refuse I would ask her for just half a cup which in Gladys speak meant and inch from the top of the cup rather than almost overflowing! Work would finish at seven o'clock after milking followed by cooked supper before cycling home. It did seem a lot of food but you certainly needed it during a twelve hour, often gruelling, day. There had been no mention about how much I was to be paid but at the end of the first six day week; it worked out at two shillings and hour. When I got home that Saturday and told mam that I thought it was a very low rate she asked me if I wanted to continue but I had no hesitation, I had absolutely loved it and of course a lot of really good food was included! I think that my pay reflected the poor level of pay that farm labourers (known in Welsh as **'Y Gwas'**) earned.

The **gwas** at Close was called John and I used to deal with him a lot as he was the one who usually told me what I had to do and how to do it. There was a lot of tidying up, repair work and clearing up especially after animals and I got to drive two of the tractors. One was a small grey Massey Ferguson, a model that was very common on farms at the time and ideal for lightweight work. I used this to cut thistles in fields which had been unused for a while so that the cattle could graze in them once the grass had grown to a reasonable height.

I also drove a vintage tractor in a ploughed field. Attached to it was a nasty looking contraption of metal spikes called a field cultivator which broke down the ploughed soil into a fine tilth ready for planting seeds. On my first day things were going well as I drove up and down the field. The tractor had no gearbox, just one speed and you put it in gear by pressing a lever forward and stopping by pulling the lever back and applying the handbrake. After one sharp turn the cultivator became a bit tangled so I stopped to straighten it out. I put the tractor out of gear, applied the brake and jumped off to straighten things up. As I was about to climb back on the tractor decided to go off on its own, I obviously hadn't applied one of the levers properly. There was nothing I could do as the tractor made its way towards the hedge. Unfortunately, or maybe fortunately, it chose a hedge which had a ditch in front and a lot of undergrowth. The tractor ploughed into the undergrowth and eventually stalled in the ditch. I was really worried when I went to look for John but fortunately found him before seeing the owner Arthur. John was great about it, I don't know if he told Arthur but no mention was made of the incident. However it was a really awkward tractor to restart which involved placing a lighted wick which looked like a glowing cigarette on the end of a short lever which had to be screwed into the front of the tractor and then he had to turn a crank handle (which could give a nasty kick back if you weren't careful) until the engine caught. John had to climb through the undergrowth to get to the front which was facing downwards partly in the wet ditch. He eventually got the wick in and after several turns the engine fired and John was able to climb on and reverse the tractor out of the hedge. Apart from the time wasted and the huge embarrassment no damage was done which was just as well as I would have probably had to work for months (or even years at my rate of pay) to cover the costs.

As it was the summer, quite a few days were spent working on the hay harvest. Bales would be collected from the fields by tractor and trailer and my job was to stack them neatly on the trailer and then, at the hay shed, either throw them down to be stacked in the barn or as the barn became fuller load them onto the conveyer belt which took them up to where they were needed. In order to keep up the necessary pace I needed help in passing the bales from the front half of the trailer because the conveyor was fed from the back of the trailer and usually this help was provided by Eirian from Oernant farm next door.

During the early part of many summers Lyndon and I, and sometimes with John Allison and Michael Adams, would work on various local farms on the hay harvest. We were popular amongst the farmers as we could do every aspect of the harvest and they didn't have to pay a full labourer's rate. We could drive tractors and lift and stack bales in the fields and in the hay barns. Driving a tractor forward wasn't a big deal but reversing a tractor and trailer full of hay was quite tricky as you had to turn the front of the trailer the opposite direction to where you wanted the back to go, but turn too sharp and you would end up in a right mess, but we could all do it. Usually when collecting a load of hay I would be on the trailer building the load while the others either drove or lifted the bales onto the trailer either by hand or using a pitchfork. There was another labourer who would often turn up looking for work and he would always be hired as he had quite a reputation in the area. He would turn up with his pitchfork and would do everything at a run. If we had a break for a cup of tea, he would either not have one or down it quickly and then go running off to move the scattered bales into piles for easier collection; no wonder he was in great demand.

Another summer job I had was labouring for a local builder and friend of the family called Ieuan Harries (he had rebuilt the gable end of our house and regularly used to help with Blaenffos Church renovations). He was a real craftsman but very slow which meant that labouring was not particularly arduous. Lyndon also had a stint working for him and Ieuan also tried to teach us some of the skills needed for his job so it was more than just labouring. During the corona virus lockdown Lyndon rebuilt the roof on the pigsty at his current home (he's not a famer but lives in an old farmhouse) and said that once he started, all the training that Ieuan Harries had given him came back to him and he really enjoyed it. Again the pay wasn't great but the work was very enjoyable. One job involved painting the gable end of a house located in the countryside not far from Boncath. The owner was called Dyfed and was, shall we say, a rather eccentric character. He was in the process of putting a cesspit in and, like dad had done, he was digging it out himself. It was a warm summer and as he was digging in clay the bottom of the cesspit was full of water. Dyfed did all the digging by hand often dressed in a bathing costume and a pair of wellingtons with holes in. He had cut the holes in his wellingtons as the depth of the water was above the top of the wellingtons but he needed something to protect his feet and when he climbed out of the pit his wellingtons would empty without having to take them off yet when he was in the pit they weren't uncomfortably full of water. The bathing costume meant that he had very few dirty clothes to wash after a day's work. Well it seemed perfectly logical to Dyfed.

One summer I got a job painting for a farmer whose farm sat at the foot of Y Frenni Fawr. This mainly involved painting the roof of a barn and even with a wide brush this took quite a bit of time. When I finished he asked me to do the same for a property he had in Crymmych which bordered onto the playing fields of Ysgol Y Preseli. Another barn roof was involved and I was left to my own devices but I was quite responsible and could get on with the job unsupervised. Mam as usual had provided a packed lunch and I spent my dinner (half) hour sat on the zinc roof under the blazing sun watching the activities on the school grounds. After finishing this job the farmer's wife asked me to paint the windows and weather boards of a house she owned in the Cardiganshire village of Penparc, situated three miles north-east of Cardigan. As it happens she owned and lived in her own property in the village and the house I was asked to paint was two doors down from hers and was let out as holiday accommodation. When I did the windows I found that there was something stuck to the edges of the frames which prevented me producing a nice finish with the gloss, so I removed it. It was only later that I found out that this was draft excluder! While on this job I didn't need a packed lunch as I was well fed and watered by the owner so it was just as well I had the key to the house which allowed me easy access to the toilet. During this job, I got quite friendly with the elderly couple next door and they asked me to paint their timberwork. They rented out a couple of rooms for bed and breakfast and would usually provide me with a cup of tea during a morning break. Unfortunately they did not possess a fridge so the milk was often off but I didn't have the heart to refuse their hospitality and always finished my cuppa and it didn't do me any harm. During this summer I was able to charge a decent hourly rate for my work which gave me a good income and the rate was happily accepted by all my 'customers'. I couldn't believe my eyes when I saw the antics of the so called professional painter who was painting the house next door. It was a bungalow with a rear extension which had a long weather board which was easily reached without a ladder. Now I was taught to clean and rub down the old paintwork if necessary and apply undercoat and gloss. Well this painter had a wide brush and was just walking along with one final coat painting over everything including all the cobwebs which were sticking to the brush as he went along. He obviously wasn't being paid by the hour.

The job that I enjoyed the most (and the best paid) was working as a labourer for a pair of plasterers. They were on the lookout for a new labourer as their latest one had only lasted a week. He was a well known local hard man from Boncath and while he was strong, he was completely unfit so struggled to keep up the pace of the work for a whole day. The plasters would drink at my Uncle Islwyn's pub usually at the end of the Friday shift and he recommended me to them, so I was taken on without an interview and without meeting them. The building site was an estate that was being built on the northern outskirts of Cardigan. On the first morning it was raining hard and I arrived early on my motor bike so I was sheltering under the roof overhang of a bungalow. There I was, five foot six inches with an oversized raincoat and crash helmet, looking like a drowned rat. A young lad, not much older than me walked past and told me that I wouldn't last a week. I wish I had seen him two months later when the work finished in Cardigan and I stayed with them while they started on some new houses in Lampeter, which is where they were from!

Although they didn't tell me until much later, when they saw me, they wondered what Islwyn had landed them with. They were unsure for much of the first week until an incident which occurred on the Friday of that week. We were laying floors in a bungalow and my job was firstly to remove rubbish from and brush out the rooms where the floors were laid, then mix the screed (sand, cement and water) in the mixer and barrow it into the rooms which had been cleared. At lunch time they said they were going into town for something to eat and wouldn't be long. As I had my own sandwiches (can you imagine mam letting me go to work without plenty of food?) I didn't need anything so I stayed on site. We usually had no more than half an hour for lunch and after an hour I thought they would be back soon and I couldn't just sit around doing nothing. So I cleaned out the next room and mixed enough screed to fill the room. Still no sign of them but I was in my first week and I wanted to make a good impression so I carried on until I had mixed enough to complete another room then thought I had better stop. When they returned mid afternoon it turned out that they had been at Islwyn's pub and were planning on an early finish. They couldn't believe it when they returned to see the piles of screed so there was no chance of an early finish as they couldn't let the screed go hard and couldn't say much as they hadn't said they were going to the pub. As it turned out I had overestimated the amount needed for the two rooms and so I had to clear another two and barrow the surplus into these two rooms. The plasterers worked like dogs and were sweating buckets and had soaking trouser legs as they had to work on their knees on the damp screed. Anyway they finished the house in record time and hopefully the finished article stood the test of time. By the time they were ready to go home they realised that I would be able to cope with labouring for two plasterers. They were also surprised that I could play five-a-side soccer with my brother and friends after work a couple of times a week. But the work and soccer kept me fit and was good summer training before the rugby season started.

As I was quite fit I could handle the weight and intensity of work but sometimes my lack of height made it difficult to handle certain equipment. In particular tipping a builder's wheelbarrow full of concrete was tricky as I had to get on my toes to tip it completely and often had to let go so that the barrow followed the cement onto the heap. A hod is a long pole with a triangular box, open on one end, attached to the top of the pole and is used to carry bricks and the concrete mix upstairs. The handle is rested on your shoulder but this was tricky for me as the handle was too long and I had to tip it up at an uncomfortable angle to stop it hitting every step on the way up. Then when I had to tip it onto the plasterer's spot (a large piece of wood sitting on trestles or on a stack of concrete blocks) control was difficult as the handle would hit against the floor and the mixture would land fairly rapidly on the spot and the plasterers had to put their trowels and hawks either side of the approaching pile to prevent it splashing on the walls. Eventually we worked out that if I stepped on top of two concrete blocks I was six feet two inches tall and the handle didn't hit the floor. I suppose we could have cut a bit off the end of the handle as this would not have mattered to average height or tall future users but none of us thought about it, so why was the handle so long in the first place?

The job of the plasterer is to come in after the skeleton of the house has been built and put the next layer onto the internal and external walls, floors and ceilings before they are painted or, in the case of floors, to make them ready for the final floor covering. This involves applying a mixture of dry goods - sand, cement, sometimes chippings or the pink plaster known as gypsum thistle plaster - and water, depending on which job is being done. As already mentioned screed is spread on the floor on top of the concrete slab, a mix of sand and cement is used as the first coat on top of internal concrete block walls and this is finished with a coat of thistle plaster and water. Plastering external walls is called rendering and this is done with a mixture of sand, cement and lime. In addition if internal walls are made of plasterboard this requires a finish of gypsum thistle plaster in the same way as the ceilings which are usually made of plasterboard. Most of these combinations can be placed in a cement mixer but the pink thistle plaster is mixed in a bucket by hand or by a mechanical whisk, in my case by hand as we didn't have the luxury of a mechanical whisk. Basically you just put in the right amount of water and thistle to get the smooth creamy consistency (a bit like thick Greek yoghurt) which will adhere to the concreted wall. It was a mad rush to mix enough and run upstairs with a bucketful to tip onto the spot before running back down to mix the next lot (downstairs is where the water was if you are wondering why I didn't mix it upstairs) as a bucketful doesn't take long to spread on the walls. However once it was on it had to be smoothed with a metal finish trowel and a wooden trowel known as a float. This took some time and I thought that this was probably one of the most difficult and skilful of all the plastering jobs but it was good for me as I had nothing to do while the smoothing and drying was going on.

I have already mentioned some of the tools used by plasterers and their labourers. Another tool called the hawk is a flat piece of wood with a handle attached underneath, the cement or plaster is drawn off the spot onto the hawk with a trowel which is then taken to the surface and applied, a straight edge piece of wood known as a screed board is often drawn over the applied product to make it smoother and if necessary a wooden float is used to give a final smooth finish.

Various types of sand, the sand/cement ratio and the amount of water gives the products different consistencies. Getting the required mix was probably the most important job I had to do. When the work finished in Cardigan I decided to go to the next job in Lampeter and that's when I bought my first car for one hundred pounds (four weeks' wages). I was paid five pounds a day for a five day week but sometimes I would go in on a Saturday morning as this is when my employers attended to the snagging list which is dealing with any little faults or defects or any small items missed. They would be paid separately by the hour for this, and so was I, even though I had very little to do.

Conclusion

So as the 1960s came to an end I went to Swansea University to study for a degree in Economics and Geography. During my third year I met my future wife and after my three year degree I did a year of teacher's training(PGCE) and in 1973 got a job teaching Economics at Cynffig Comprehensive School in Kenfig Hill near Bridgend, followed by my marriage to Joanne in 1974. During the 1970s I played rugby for Bridgend, Maesteg and Cardiff before retiring in 1979 to spend more time with Joanne and to start a family. We have been blessed with two smashing daughters Rachel and Emma and years later with four fabulous grand-children, Megan, Huw, Eva and Jessica. Lockdowns permitting, the family now takes up most of our time and we wouldn't have it any other way.

Memories of my early years at Brynislwyn in West Wales may have faded slightly but they will always be with me and writing this book has brought to the fore many happy memories in particular the freedom, friendships, experiences and richness of life, despite being financially poor; these being the various influences which have helped to shape my character and my life. I am a glass half full person and I like to think that the grounding for that was laid in my extremely happy upbringing.

ABOUT THE AUTHOR

The author was born and bred in West Wales into a way of life that seems alien to modern times. After his A levels he studied at Swansea University for four years before being appointed, in 1973, as Economics Teacher at Cynffig Comprehensive School in the county of Glamorgan. After thirty-five years at the school he retired from the post of Assistant Head. He now lives in a small village outside Bridgend with his wife Joanne. He was inspired to write this book by the fond memories of his upbringing, the prompting of his family and the corona virus lockdown of 2020.

Printed in Great Britain
by Amazon